I0189385

IMAGES
of America

BELVIDERE AND
BOONE COUNTY

ON THE COVER: Belvidere fire chief Frank Clark, center, joined the fire department in 1903 and swiftly worked his way up to become chief on May 1, 1907. He retired on October 16, 1946, after serving for 39 years. During his time with the department, Clark responded to more than 3,000 fire alarms. Standing next to him is fireman Bay Strong; the driver is unidentified. (Courtesy of the Boone County Historical Museum.)

IMAGES
of America

BELVIDERE AND BOONE COUNTY

The Boone County History Project

ARCADIA
PUBLISHING

Copyright © 2015 by the Boone County History Project
ISBN 978-1-5316-7129-7

Published by Arcadia Publishing
Charleston, South Carolina

Library of Congress Control Number: 2014958792

For all general information, please contact Arcadia Publishing:
Telephone 843-853-2070
Fax 843-853-0044
E-mail sales@arcadiapublishing.com
For customer service and orders:
Toll-Free 1-888-313-2665

Visit us on the Internet at www.arcadiapublishing.com

CONTENTS

ACKNOWLEDGMENTS

The Boone County History Project would like to thank the following people and institutions for their help with this project. We are deeply grateful to the board of directors and staff at the Boone County Historical Museum for the use of its collections; all images appearing in this book were provided by the Boone County Historical Museum, unless otherwise noted. A thank-you also goes to the Ida Public Library for the use of its Local History Room's research materials and collections. Special thanks go to Debbie Bloom, director of the Ida Public Library, for encouraging this project to go forward.

Thank you, to the *Belvidere Daily Republican* newspaper, particularly Lisa Paulsen Rodgers, for helping us promote this project. We would like to thank Louise Hawkey Miles and the Wolf family for offering us the use of their personal photographs. We appreciate those who assisted project members in some capacity throughout this process, especially George Gibson, George Thomas, Maurice Ernest, and Nathan Fuller. Finally, we would like to express gratitude for the support and encouragement we received from the entire Boone County community. We are honored to help promote this county's history and heritage.

INTRODUCTION

To understand who we are, we need to understand where we have been, and that is the purpose of Images of America: *Belvidere and Boone County*. Boone County, one of the northernmost counties in Illinois, is bordered by suburban Chicago, the Rockford metropolitan area, and the state of Wisconsin. Residents are fiercely proud of their community, one of the fastest-growing counties in the state and nation from 2000 to 2010. Boone County is defined by its landmarks such as the 1837 Baltic Mill in Belvidere, its cultural and historical events like the Boone County Fair, and its institutions, including the Boone County Historical Museum. The original settlers were attracted to Boone County's agricultural potential, and the county remains rooted in that agricultural heritage.

Boone County was named after Daniel Boone, the famous pioneer, though he never came to this area of Illinois. The county consists of nine townships, from the wooded reaches of Manchester and Leroy to the prairie townships of Spring and Flora, named to reflect their landscapes. In between are the townships of Caledonia, Poplar Grove, Boone, Belvidere, and Bonus. Belvidere has historically been the largest city, and over time, people have settled in the communities of Caledonia, Poplar Grove, Capron, Garden Prairie, Russellville, Newburg, Lawrenceville, Argyle, Herbert, Irene, Blaine, and Hunter.

Today, a trip to Chicago takes less than two hours by car. When settlement opened in Illinois in the 1830s, those traveling from Chicago to the Rock River Valley region by foot or wagon would have endured a three-day trek. The first settlers to Boone County found a well-watered prairie thanks to waterways that included the Kishwaukee River. Settlers also encountered Native Americans who found this area bountiful for hunting, fishing, and planting. There is documented evidence that the Potawatomie tribe camped in the southern and eastern parts of the county. The Potawatomie also moved through the county on their way to other areas, using what is now US Route 20 as their "interstate."

Following the Black Hawk War of 1832, the first pioneers began to arrive in 1835. Some of the earliest pioneers included John Langdon, Livingston Robbins, Archibald Metcalf, John Handy, and David Dunham. That same year, John Towner, Cornelius Cline, and Erastus Nixon decided to settle in the area after meeting up with Metcalf and Dunham, who were camped out on the banks of the Kishwaukee River. Towner, who had intended to go on to Rockford, declared, "Others, expecting to find a paradise on the Rock River, may go there; as for me, I go no further."

The next wave of settlement began that same year with Simon P. Doty, Ebenezer Peck, Daniel Whitney, and Josiah Goodhue. Utilizing the Kishwaukee River as a resource, the first industry of grist- and sawmills was established. Boone County continued to attract industry well into the latter part of the 19th century and early 20th century. Some successful companies included the Gossard Corset Factory, Longcor's Plow Works, and the National Sewing Machine Company. Yesterday's industries still impact the county today; the Keene Canning Company has now become Green Giant, while Borden's Condensed Milk Company is now Dean Foods. Agriculture also contributed to the county's economic development. Boone County has rich soil as a result of the last glacial period; when the glaciers receded, they left behind nutrient-rich soil, as well as exposed limestone quarries, which provided foundations for many of the early homes in Belvidere and the rest of the county. Three of the early crops grown here were corn, soybeans, and wheat. Dairy farms were another common enterprise, and the establishment of many creameries capitalized on the proliferation of Boone County dairy farms.

New modes of transportation into the county influenced how and when people emigrated here. Not long after the county was settled, Belvidere and Garden Prairie (then Amesville) became stops on the stagecoach route from Chicago to Galena. Besides the New Englanders coming into the county, the first wave of immigration brought the Norwegians, who settled in the northern townships. Tennis Tollefson was most likely the first Norwegian to settle here, in 1836. Scottish immigrants also arrived around that time and settled in Scotch Grove, on the border of Boone and Winnebago Counties. The next large wave of immigration brought the Irish, who arrived with the railroad in the early 1850s. They settled in Belvidere near the railroad tracks in such large numbers that the neighborhood became known as the Irish Patch. Their presence led to the establishment of St. James Catholic Church.

Life in the 19th century was centered on the farm and the rural community. The church and the one-room schoolhouse provided social outlets, and businesses were small and specialized. Because of the limitations of transportation, people tended to stay where their roots were. As the county moved into the 20th century, growth was inevitable. Larger and more diversified industries, centralized education, and faster transportation contributed to the modernization of daily life for all residents.

Although it is located near Rockford and Chicago, Boone County was more geographically isolated than it is today. However, local and national events still affected the county and forced it to make changes. The Civil War and several economic panics of the late 19th century had a great effect on both the county as a whole and on individual citizens. The major events of the 20th century, such as World War I, Prohibition, the Roaring Twenties, and the Great Depression also impacted the culture and growth of the county, opening the door to further change in the post–World War II era.

In its first 100 years, Boone County has been the home of a major-league baseball player, several Civil War generals, a world-class sewing machine industry, a Frank Lloyd Wright chapel, and a nurse who gave her life during World War I, as well as countless citizens who have contributed to the county's growth and success. Then and now, Boone County's residents have had a deep pride in their community, heritage, and future.

One

SETTLEMENT ON

THE PRAIRIE

In 1835, settlers began to build log cabins and stake land in what was to become Boone County, Illinois. Most of these pioneers came from the East; they must have been amazed at the prairie stretching to the horizon and the abundance of clear flowing waterways.

Of course, the pioneers were not the first people to inhabit Boone County. Native Americans, mostly of the Potawatomie tribe, used the land to plant crops, fish, hunt, and trap. The first Europeans here were trappers passing through. US Army troops under Gen. Winfield Scott also came through the county while chasing Black Hawk and his warriors.

By 1835, the relentless flow of settlers moving west found land to be settled in the extreme northern part of Illinois. Most of them came from Chicago and found the trek to Boone County a formidable one, sloshing through rivers and streams on wagons pulled by horses or oxen. In that year, John Handy became the first to plant his feet in Spring Township, and John Towner arrived on the banks of the Kishwaukee River with Cornelius Cline and Erastus Nixon to found what would become Belvidere. James Sawyer claimed land on Beaver Creek, upstream from the Kishwaukee, where he would build the first mill. That same year, Simon Doty and Dr. Daniel Whitney came to an encampment on the river and pooled their resources with Dr. Josiah Goodhue, Ebenezer Peck, and Nathaniel Crosby to establish a permanent settlement.

Other outposts became settlements as more immigrants arrived to stake claims on the prairie. Some early settlers became restless again and moved on, replaced by others seeking their share of Boone County's bounty. The communities of Newburg and Russellville came and went, while other communities, such as Garden Prairie, grew when the railroad came in the 1850s. Those who left and those who stayed helped give birth to the county of today.

Henry Sweet was the first white male born in Boone County and may have been the first white child. Sweet was born on September 15, 1837, in Bonus Township to parents who arrived in 1836 with the first wave of settlers. Sweet, a lifelong bachelor, was active in the county throughout his life. He died of a heart attack on December 5, 1907, at age 70, while working in his yard.

In early 1835, John Towner arrived in Boone County and built a log cabin, then returned to Michigan to retrieve his family. They returned by way of Chicago, with Towner walking the oxen while his wife, Hannah Loop Towner, drove the wagon. They arrived at the banks of the Kishwaukee at midnight on July 31, 1835, establishing Hannah as the first female settler of European heritage in the region.

In 1836, Charles McDougall and two other men arrived in Boone County from Quebec, Canada, bringing the first merchandise to the county. Goods such as coffee, sugar, and cloth were purchased in New York or Boston, then shipped to Chicago via the Erie Canal and Great Lakes. The goods were then transferred to ox-drawn wagons for the three-day trip to Boone County in exchange for eggs, milk products, and beef.

Hannah Molony Blake, born in the East, immigrated to Boone County with her family in 1844. The Molonys came from Lime, New Hampshire, and Hannah's brother Richard became a doctor. The family established strong roots locally, and in her later years, Hannah talked extensively about her pioneer life. Hannah, who died at the age of 93 in 1905, was well respected and said to be of "strong mentality."

Some of the first homes constructed in the county were rural log cabins. The photograph above, featuring several women in their Sunday best, was likely taken in Flora Township. The photograph below was taken on land eventually owned by Henry Zoellick, who came to Boone County from Wisconsin. The cabin stood in Manchester Township near the Wisconsin border. It was a challenge for pioneers to find wood on the Boone County prairie for their cabins. Those first to arrive in the central and southern prairies settled land along the Kishwaukee River or along creeks, as oaks in the nearby savannas provided needed lumber.

Rivers were the superhighways and semiconductors of the 19th century, providing transportation and industrial potential. The original settlers of Belvidere were naturally drawn to the Kishwaukee River. In August 1835, five men invested $10,000 to build grist- and sawmills. By the next year, they built the Crosby sawmill on the river. In 1837, another mill was built to grind grain. Eventually, the county had 12 mills. In 1845, the Crosby Mill was rebuilt for $12,000 and became the Baltic Mill. This photograph shows the Baltic Mill, which operated as a gristmill until 1918. The mill today is part of Belvidere Park. In the 1990s, it was renovated and has become a public gathering place. The mill is perhaps the most photographed landmark in the county, which befits the oldest building in the area.

Ames Tavern began as a stop on the Frink and Walker stagecoach trail that ran from Chicago to Galena. In 1836, William Ames opened a tavern in his home. It took five days to travel by stage from Chicago to Boone County, and this was the only stop between Elgin and Belvidere. With business booming, Ames added a trading post and general store to his residence. When Ames died, he left the prosperous business to his son George. When the railroad came through in the 1850s, George saw it as a threat to his business, although his property was on the projected right-of-way. After George refused the offer to become a depot agent, the railroad built a depot a quarter of a mile east of the tavern in what was to become Garden Prairie. Stagecoach service ended in 1853, and the tavern closed for good in 1860. The building still stands, with a stone plaque marking its historical significance.

Hawkey's Barn stood on land owned by Robert R. Hawkey, a prominent farmer and county board member, and located on old Illinois Route 5 (now US 20), near Irene Road. The barn was from the early village of Newburg, founded in 1835 by James Sayre. The Reverend James O'May painted the barn about 1946. (Courtesy of Louise Hawkey Miles.)

Nature blessed southern Boone County with durable limestone, and quarries in Belvidere provided the foundations for most of the communities' early homes. At that time, it was common to see horse-drawn wagons like those in this photograph hauling stone into Belvidere. One stone taken from here was reported to be six feet wide, 21 feet long, and three inches thick.

15

Simon P. Doty is a remarkable figure in Boone County history. When Doty and Dr. Daniel Whitney arrived on the banks of the Kishwaukee River in August 1835, they bought a claim and built a small cabin. Over time, Doty became a respected citizen, serving as the county's first sheriff in 1837, using a room of his home as the first jail, running a ferry after a flood washed out the first bridge over the Kishwaukee River in 1840, and representing local citizens as the first state legislator for Boone County. Doty also operated the Belvidere House, the county's first hotel and first framed building. The hotel was located on the Chicago and Galena stagecoach route on the corner of North State and Mechanic (now Lincoln Avenue) Streets and held the county's first liquor license. Doty was tall and muscular, posed ramrod-straight for photographs, and told stories of the good old days until his death.

This photograph of the south bank of the Kishwaukee in 1870 shows Austin's Livery Barn (left) and the Doty Hotel (right), as well as the fourth bridge at State Street. The first two bridges were swept away by spring floods in 1840 and 1845. The third, a covered bridge, was replaced in 1867 by this one, which was built of latticed iron and cost $15,000.

Started in 1848, the Galena & Chicago Union Railroad reached Garden Prairie in 1851 and arrived in Belvidere by the next year. The line, originally planned for the north side of the Kishwaukee River, was built on the south side in a business deal crafted by William Holt Gilman. This pioneer railroad eventually became the Chicago & North Western Railway.

Norwegian immigration to Boone County began in 1842, when two Norwegian pioneers settled in northeastern Boone County. A year later, they were joined by Endre Stimes and others who were originally headed to Wiota, Wisconsin. In 1851, Endre's brother Ole joined him. This photograph, taken at the Stimes's farm in Capron in 1894, shows Ole, his wife, Olene, and their 14 children.

The beards are long and the faces time-worn at the Old Settlers' Picnic in Capron in 1893, which celebrated the pioneers who arrived from Norway beginning in the 1840s. This photograph includes Ole Tillerson, who emigrated from Voss-Bergen, Norway, in 1846. He built a log cabin on Jefferson Prairie and walked to Dixon to claim his land, for which he paid $1.25 an acre.

Two

Faces of Boone County

A place is defined by its people, and the people of Boone County are and have always been examples of the diversity found in the United States. While namesake Daniel Boone never set foot on the county's rolling prairie, his frontier spirit, determination, and caring nature fits its residents' past and present.

The county's first 100 years have produced many unique individuals, from outstanding men who led soldiers in battle to a woman who captured fugitives as an acting sheriff. John Lawson escaped slavery to fight for the Union in the Civil War. John Wesley Powell, who lived on a farm in Bonus Township as a child, lost his right arm in a Civil War battle but overcame the disability to navigate the Colorado River and become a noted scientific explorer of the Old West. Boone County produced other Civil War heroes, including two generals and a woman who disguised herself as a man.

While some upheld the law, others broke it, like Julia Stott, who coerced her lover, Dr. Thomas Cream, to murder her husband, Daniel, in 1881. Others led quiet but significant lives. Cornelia "Auntie" Wright dispensed medicine and took care of the sick and elderly in northwestern Boone County in the 19th century. Although she did not have a medical degree, Auntie Wright studied journals and relied on her instincts to make house calls with her white horse and buggy and her black medical bag.

For better or for worse, these are the people from the past who made Boone County residents who they are today.

Pvt. Albert D.J. Cashier (right) survived several major Civil War engagements, including the Siege of Vicksburg and the Battle of Nashville, in the 95th Illinois Infantry Volunteers. More than 30 years later, it was revealed that Cashier was actually a woman, Jennie Hodgers. At five-foot-three-inches tall and 110 pounds, Cashier appeared healthy enough to enlist in the army, which did not give physicals. Hodgers emigrated from Ireland, where she had worked on her father's farm with her twin brother and often wore his clothes. After immigrating to America, she arrived in Belvidere and enlisted as a man in Company G of the 95th Regiment, perhaps for the $13 monthly pay. Cashier kept up the masquerade until 1900, when an illness unveiled her secret. She spent her final days in a soldiers' and sailors' home, as well as an insane asylum, before dying in 1913. Her grave has two headstones—one for Jennie Hodgers, the other for Albert Cashier, proof of one of the Civil War's most intriguing stories.

Southern-born, he settled in Illinois, practiced law, and got into politics. That description fits Abraham Lincoln as well as Stephen Hurlbut of Belvidere, who became a friend of the president. Hurlbut's name was the first on the list when President Lincoln called for army volunteers in 1860. Eventually, Hurlbut was promoted to major general of the 4th Army Division of the Army of the Tennessee. On April 7, 1862, at the Battle of Shiloh, Hurlbut spurred on his troops at the Peach Orchard, also known as the Hornet's Nest. After the war, he helped organize the Grand Army of the Republic (GAR) society and served as its first national commander. Hurlbut was elected to the state legislature and eventually became the minister to Peru, where he died in 1882. One of his least-known exploits was a pre–Civil War clandestine mission for the newly elected Lincoln; the president sent Hurlbut to his hometown of Charleston, South Carolina, to see if there were any Union supporters in the South and any means of appealing to them. Hurlbut reported back that war was inevitable.

Allen Fuller came to Belvidere from Connecticut in 1846 to practice law and became a circuit judge in 1861. During the Civil War, he was appointed the adjutant general of Illinois and was the commanding officer for all Illinois troops. After the war, he became a civic leader and was elected to the state senate and house of representatives.

Born to pioneer parents in Garden Prairie, Washington Porter enlisted in the 95th Infantry Regiment at the age of 16 and was wounded at the Battle of Guntown. After the war, he invested in real estate in Chicago, where he became a wealthy civic leader. Porter, who was championed as a possible Chicago mayoral candidate, helped to organize the Chicago World's Fair in 1893.

Born a slave in Virginia in 1829, John Lawson stole a mule during the Civil War and escaped to the North, joining the 16th US Colored Infantry. After the war, he came to Boone County, where he eventually became the custodian at the Pearl Street School. He is well known for rescuing a child playing on the nearby train tracks, grabbing her just before a train rumbled by.

In 1882, Boone County sheriff Albert T. Ames appointed his wife, Sarah, as his chief deputy. After Albert fell ill at the end of his last term, Sarah replaced him as sheriff and became a crime-fighting leader, tracking down escaped criminals from the county jail, uncovering an attempted jailbreak, and thwarting unruly thugs in a courthouse hallway at gunpoint. She was also an entrepreneur and operated a hat shop in downtown Belvidere.

After William H. Durham, pictured here with his wife, Emaline, ran the Garden Prairie School for $15 a month, he became Boone County's first superintendent of schools in 1866. He later represented Bonus Township at the state convention in 1864 that nominated Pres. Abraham Lincoln to run for a second term. Born in 1832, Durham died in Chicago in September 1926.

Born on a prairie farm in 1849, Charles Fuller was admitted to the bar at the age of 21 and became Boone County state's attorney, a circuit court judge, and an elected member of both state legislative houses. In 1902, he was elected to the US House of Representatives. "Our own Charlie" Fuller was the featured speaker at the dedication of the Belvidere Soldiers and Sailors Memorial on October 15, 1910.

Ellen and Charles Bennett, married in 1868, pose here with their family of 12 children, six boys and six girls. Bennett was born in Flora Township and became president of the Boone County Fire Insurance Company and a leader of the South Baptist Church. They both died in 1917: Charles in South Dakota and Ellen in Pullman, Washington, where she was visiting her daughters.

William Soost was born in Prussia and ran a meat market in Belvidere before opening Soost's Bowling Alley on Buchanan Street in the early years of the 20th century. Soost's featured pool and billiard tables when it opened in 1908, and it also had a large stock of cigars. Here, he sits for a portrait with his wife, Etta, and their children—from left to right, Avis, Carl, Pearl, and Martha.

From left to right are Maggie and Katie Chamberlain and their cousin Mamie Lang, who posed for this portrait in the late 1880s. The Chamberlains' parents ran the Chamberlain Hotel in Caledonia. As an adult, Maggie was in charge of the rooms and waited tables in the restaurant, while Katie cooked with her mother. They both lived at the hotel until their deaths in 1963 and 1971, respectively.

From left to right, Elizabeth Walters, Ann Walters, and Agnes Walters enjoyed a train ride on their father's train in the backyard of their home on Union Avenue. Barney Walters spent years building the miniature locomotive and three railroad cars, which he planned to display at the Boone County Fair. From left to right in the background are Barney's wife, Jennie Walters, Carrie Avery, and a Mrs. Clark.

In 1890, Piel's Grocery Store opened on South State Street in Belvidere. William H. Piel stood out due to his innovative marketing techniques such as purchasing an entire railcar of Monarch coffee. In the 1920s, Piel started one of his most successful marketing ideas: every Christmas he ordered a massive wheel of cheese, which often sold within a week.

The businessmen and entrepreneurs of the county contributed heavily to its growth. After starting his journalistic career in 1892, Frank T. Moran (right) took over the *Belvidere Daily Republican* in 1894 and was its editor and publisher until his death in 1949. Omar Wright (left) founded a lumber company in 1889 and branched out to deal in grain and coal.

Innovative and creative, Barnabas Eldredge was a successful manufacturer, serving as president of the National Sewing Machine Company from 1890 until his death in 1911. As president, he had the knack of tapping into a trend; besides sewing machines, he started manufacturing bicycles and automobiles as they became popular. He was also known to be a man of integrity and generous to his community.

Following Frank Church and Maude Willard's wedding at the Willard home on 521 North State Street in July 1914, the couple moved to Sandusky, Ohio. Frank, who studied in France, composed organ music and performed concerts in the United States and Europe. He was a music professor at six colleges, including Baylor University. After Frank's death, Maude taught science at Belvidere High School.

Eight staff members of the Julien Hotel are pictured here, including three African Americans. While it was common for African Americans to work in Belvidere, few made it their residence. The 1890 census lists only 42 African Americans in Belvidere, which had a total population of 12,161. That number continued to grow however, leading to more diversity throughout the county.

Manuel and Alexandra Martinez headed the first Hispanic family to establish roots in Boone County. Manuel, who came from Mexico, worked for the Chicago & North Western Railway and arrived in Belvidere sometime in the late 1920s or early 1930s. The family lived on McKinley Avenue, and their children were the first Hispanics to enroll in public school in the county.

FRED SCHULTE

Fred Schulte was Boone County's most successful athlete, playing major-league baseball in the 1920s and 1930s. Schulte starred in three sports at Belvidere High School, but baseball was not one of them, since it was not yet offered. As a professional, he faced hall-of-famers Babe Ruth, Dizzy Dean, and Lou Gehrig while playing for the St. Louis Browns, the Pittsburgh Pirates, and the Washington Senators. On July 4, 1933, the Senators swept a doubleheader from the New York Yankees at Yankee Stadium before 72,000 fans. They won the first game 1-0 on Schulte's RBI; he had a key defensive play in the second game. He also hit a three-run homer in the fifth game of the 1933 World Series against the New York Giants to tie the score at 3-3. In the 10th inning, Schulte appeared to have caught Mel Ott's long shot to center field when he fell over a fence. But it was a home run and proved to be the winning run in the series.

Three

On the Homestead

Boone County's homes are as diverse as the county itself. From the earliest log cabins to the first frame houses and on to the elaborate mansions of General Hurlbut and John Crocker Foote, local houses help tell the story of Boone County.

Many early houses were extraordinarily well constructed and still stand today. The early settlers built large farms and homesteads, often with their bare hands. Others commissioned contractors and builders to construct their homes for them. Some early homes were built of limestone; a few of these still stand in Belvidere near Courthouse Square. Later, homes conformed to architectural styles from back East, such as the Gilman house on Buchanan Street. This house was built in 1851 in the Italianate style, with walls that were 20 inches thick. The Gilmans were known for signaling their relatives from the cupola on top of the house. Some houses have received expansions or additions over the years, while others have been lost to the wrecking ball. Those that still stand serve as a glimpse of old Boone County.

Life at home was often very difficult. Early residents not only had to be physically tough but mentally tough as well. For example, John Plane was a well-known hardware store owner in Belvidere. In 1858, when he was just 36 years old, he lost both his wife and a baby to consumption. He later lost his daughter Daisy at age 25 and another wife many years later. Life's intimate moments of births, deaths, celebrations, and sorrows were all experienced at home. This chapter explores the home lives of Boone County's citizens and the stories that lie within the walls.

Built by Edward Stewart Cortwright, this log cabin served as the home for the Moore family. The two-story home was located on the south side of Route 173, a quarter mile east of the early settlement of Poplar Grove. Pictured from left to right are Mr. Moore, Ella May Moore, Mrs. Moore, and two unidentified people.

These three unidentified women take a break from their daily work to pose outside their farmhouse. Farm life for women at home carried many responsibilities and long hours. Women were often responsible for making and repairing the family clothing, tending the garden, caring for the family, maintaining the home, and preparing and storing food. Women were also occasionally expected to lend a hand in the fields.

Pictured here is the farm and homestead of Daniel R. Andrus and his wife, Mary. The farm was located on the corner of Woodstock and Grange Hall Roads in Bonus Township. Life on a farm in the mid-to-late 1800s was extremely difficult. It took many hours of labor to produce even a bushel of corn or wheat. Without modern tractors and technology, farmers relied on horses and their own hands to plow, sow, and raise crops on their fields. Andrus is considered to be among the first to settle in Boone County, and he arrived in 1842. He farmed the land for 45 years before retiring and moving to Belvidere.

The Lambert family's Greek Revival farmhouse was located on Bloods Point Road in Flora Township. Born on February 14, 1870, Warren D. Lambert and his wife, Martha, farmed the land near Bloods Point Cemetery for more than 40 years. In addition to farming, Lambert was a prominent member of the Belvidere Park Board, director of the Farmer's Co-Operative Elevator Company, ran a livestock company, and oversaw the Bloods Point Cemetery.

The Jury family farm, pictured here with a child in the barnyard, is typical of a Boone County farm in the early 1900s, with barns, storage facilities, and a windmill. Windmills were typically used to power agricultural machinery such as sawmills and water pumps, which brought water from aquifers to feed livestock. This farm was likely located near Poplar Grove.

Standing in front of the Porter house are, from left to right, Gertrude (Porter) Bennett, Gladys (Porter) Dodson, Spencer Porter, and Harry Porter. The Porter family home, built in 1868, is located in Garden Prairie on Marengo Road, between Garden Prairie and County Line Roads. Multiple generations of the family have lived on and farmed the land from 1843 to the present.

This country house in Spring Township was home to George Reed for more than 50 years. In 1849, Reed purchased 120 acres of land from the government to start his first of two farms. In addition to the farms, he owned a creamery, a butter and cheese manufacturing business, and was a stockholder in the People's Bank of Belvidere. He also served on many county and state boards of agriculture.

Looking east down Logan Avenue from Whitney Boulevard, this view provides a unique image of Logan Avenue as it appeared around 100 years ago. The house at center right will be instantly recognizable as the Belvidere Funeral Home. Built in 1896, the house was originally the residence of Josiah R. Balliet. Balliet was a prominent business leader in early Belvidere. He opened a piano

store, formed the Belvidere Electric Light Company, and was involved in bringing the National Sewing Machine Company to Belvidere. The First United Methodist Church is on the left, while the Belvidere Congregational Church, built in 1906, can be seen in the distance.

Built in 1837, the Lampert Wildflower house was the first frame house built in Belvidere, constructed in the Upright and Wing architectural style. The house was purchased by Philip and Clara Lampert in 1891, and they had a daughter named Muriel in 1892. Muriel and Clara, pictured here on May 31, 1897, shared a love of nature. They planted many wildflowers and perennials on the site, which earned it the nickname of the Wildflower House. In addition to the Lamperts, the house has been home to many prominent Belvidere residents, including Dan Caswell, Daniel H. Whitney, Aaron Whitney, Seth Whitman, James Loop, Col. Joel Walker, and Ezra May. The house still stands today at 410 East Lincoln Avenue, and many of the plant species the Lamperts planted can still be seen on the property. The home was added to the National Register of Historic Places in 1988.

Several generations of the Lewis family pose in front of their house during this family gathering. The house was located near the current site of the YMCA at 230 West Locust Street. John Lewis, pictured in the center with a beard, was a contractor who arrived in Belvidere with his wife, Isabella Styles, in 1866. As a contractor, Lewis built many houses in Belvidere until his death in 1912.

A young Warren C. Rowan stands here in front of his house in Belvidere with his hoop toy. Rowan later served in World War I. This beautiful Queen Anne house was built in 1893 by Rowan's mother, Rose. The house was located at 304 South State Street near the site of the current Boone County Historical Museum; it was torn down by 1975.

In 1864, Gen. Stephen Hurlbut built this massive three-story mansion at 534 East Hurlbut Avenue. The street at that time was known as East Street. The house was built in the Italianate style and featured an arched front door and 20 rooms, including a dancing room on the third floor. It was torn down in 1937.

This grand house was built in 1913 by well-respected Belvidere pharmacist John Crocker Foote. Still standing at 303 East Lincoln Avenue, this Prairie-style home contains 20 rooms. The house was built with many modern amenities such as walk-in closets and conduit wiring. Foote lived here with his wife, Helen, until his death in 1917.

The Woodruff house, pictured here, was built around 1860 in the Italianate style. Charles and Harriet Woodruff operated it as a boardinghouse for nearly 28 years, with great success. The house was originally located at 210 South State Street, on the current site of the post office building, but was moved across the street in 1911. It was torn down in 2000.

This bedroom in the home of Drs. Alden and Annie Alguire represents a typical bedroom of early Belvidere. Both medical doctors, the Alguires ran a medical practice in Belvidere from 1908 until 1937. Note the power cord running from the lamp to the wall. Electric light was first introduced to Belvidere in 1877. Initially, the utility was used only for Christmas services at local churches, but it eventually expanded to homes and businesses.

The Dunton family poses for a photograph in front of their home located at 807 McKinley Avenue in Belvidere. Beautifully constructed in the Greek Revival style, the house was built by Asa Baldwin around 1850. George Dunton purchased the house in 1863. The house was originally a farmhouse outside of the city limits but is now part of a residential neighborhood. It stayed in the Dunton family until 1920.

This well-decorated and furnished room in Barnabas Eldredge's house serves as a good example of upscale interior design in early Belvidere. The house was built in the late 1880s at 513 Pearl Street, near the intersection of Pleasant Street. It was demolished in 1966 after a fire. Eldredge served as president of the National Sewing Machine Company from 1890 until his death in 1911.

Four

DOING BUSINESS

Most of Boone County's initial settlers were farmers, which in the early days was a tremendous amount of work. The invention of threshing machines and, eventually, steam engines significantly helped the farmers become more efficient in the late 19th century.

The first shops that typically opened in rural communities were essential-need stores such as general stores, blacksmiths, hardware, dry goods, and feed stores. By the early 1900s, the stores in Boone County started to become more specialized. The main streets of the towns and villages of the county became commercial centers, featuring everything from ice-cream parlors to law offices.

As the years went on, industry in Boone County began to thrive. Large factories such as the Capron Tile Factory, Belvidere Screw and Machine Company, and the Sanitary Scale Company saw great success well into the 1900s. In 1886, the June Manufacturing Company opened its doors in Belvidere. That company later became known as the National Sewing Machine Company and was the largest employer in Belvidere, with more than 2,500 workers. The dairy industry was another important facet of Boone County's economy, and the county was home to more than 15 creameries throughout the late 1800s and early 1900s. The success of the local creameries brought larger creameries into the county, such as Bowman's Dairy and the New York Milk Condensing Company.

The vision and hard work of early businessmen and farmers were essential to the success of the county. Their efforts served as the building blocks to create the county people see today.

Farming was essential to the development of Boone County, and one of the most common crops in those early days was wheat. Threshing machines, like the ones shown here, made the process of separating the grain from the stalk a lot easier. The machines were animal-powered, but the farmers still had to feed the machine by hand. The farmers fed the wheat stalks into the hopper, which controlled the amount of grain in the machine. The machine then separated the grain from the stalk. Pictured below is a threshing crew on the Thomas Blachford farm in Spring Township in 1898.

Like many early residents of Boone County, Edward Barringer and his parents moved to the area to make a living on the prairie. Barringer was born on September 5, 1856, in Albany, New York. His 80-acre farm was located in Spring Township at the intersection of Johnson and Chrysler Roads, just north of the current I-90 toll road. Barringer operated his farm until 1906, when he moved to Belvidere.

Steam engines, like those pictured here, greatly improved efficiency on the farm. The self-propelled steam engines were able to move larger loads, pull plows, and provide stationary power to threshing machines. Due to the high cost of these machines, many smaller farmers pooled funds and shared a steam engine. Steam engines were most popular in the late 1800s and early 1900s before being replaced by cheaper gas engines.

A. Gates White of Garden Prairie built this grain elevator next to his lumber and feed business in 1901. Grain elevators were very common in Boone County, particularly in towns located along the railroad. Wood-cribbed grain elevators like the one pictured carried the grain from the bottom level and then loaded it into bins or other storage devices. The grain was then transported by rail to cities such as Chicago.

After coming to Belvidere in 1905, Charles Platt Helligas (right) worked for the Watkins Company of Winona, Minnesota, as a Watkins man. Watkins men took their wagons door-to-door selling Watkins all-natural medical supplies. The Helligas family, posing here at the corner of Eighth Street and Whitney Boulevard, includes Charles, his wife, Mabel, and their children Marcia, Floreita, Mabel, Ruth, Clyde, and Emory.

Pictured here is Blaine Creamery in Leroy Township. The wagons in the foreground were used for picking up full milk cans from the local farms or taking milk to their customers. The creameries pasteurized the milk they received from the farmers and then delivered it. More milk was reserved for making cottage cheese, cheese, butter, and buttermilk. Creameries were an important industry in the early days of Boone County, and the first creamery was owned by Frank Munn in 1876. Other creameries in the late 1800s included ones at Blood's Point, Irene, and Argyle, as well as the C.M. Wait Company, Coleman's, and Borden's. The success of these small creameries attracted the attention of larger companies. Bowman Dairy Company of Chicago opened a location in Herbert in 1918 and produced over 20,000 gallons of milk per day.

This photograph, taken in 1859, shows how downtown Poplar Grove appeared to early pioneers. In this view of the south side of town, a grocery store and blacksmith shop can be seen. Poplar Grove was first settled in the late 1830s and named for the abundance of poplar trees found near the rail depot. F. Willis Edgell served as the first mayor in 1876.

In this view of Main Street in downtown Capron, Robert V. Johnson's general store, complete with a turret, can be seen at left. Downtown Capron was also home to a number of other businesses, such as Goodall's hardware store, B.L. Benson's store, Westerman's Grocery, Olsen's Drug Store, the Capron Bank, Fallon's Barber Shop, Martinsen's Blacksmith, and many more. The village was first settled in 1830s and incorporated in 1873.

The town of Herbert was established in Spring Township as people began to settle near one of the county's railroad stops. Daniel Bathrick, who owned the land and granted the right-of-way to the railroad, named the settlement Herbert after his son. By the early 1900s, the village was visited daily by passenger and coal trains, and a number of businesses sprang up near the railroad depot. There was a stockyard, contractor, church, lumberyard, telephone exchange, pickle factory, grain elevator, post office, two general stores, two blacksmiths, two creameries, and an implement dealer. Here, the Powell family poses in front of Herbert's general store and post office.

Even before the days of the automobile, South State Street served as one of the main business centers of Belvidere. On South State Street, one could find a number of specialized stores to meet one's needs, including clothing, shoes, hats, hardware stores, dry goods, groceries, a doctor, a lawyer, a piano store, and much more.

John Krieger (inside) and William Butcher (outside) operated a feed store at 215–217 North State Street. Krieger, who also served as an alderman and chief of police, teamed up with his father-in-law, Butcher, to buy a feed store from George D. Brush in 1907. They sold hay bales, straw, salt, plants, incubators, and various livestock feed.

Ray's Hardware was started in 1900 when William W. Ray and his brothers bought out the previous firm of Livingstone and Buchanan. Like many hardware stores at the time, the store carried tinware, stoves, bicycles, tools, and also paints and oils. Many of these items can be seen in this interior photograph. A paint and varnish catalog can be seen on the front counter on the left. The hardware store was located at 409 South State Street, and the building still exists today. In addition to owning his hardware store, Ray was also a prominent member of the Methodist church and served two terms as Belvidere's mayor. He ran without opposition and was first elected in 1915 and served until 1919. Ray had been a resident of Belvidere for over 75 years when he passed away in 1932.

Gooch's grocery and general store was located in Garden Prairie. Before opening his own store, Frank Gooch worked in a number of general stores and groceries, including William H. Piel's. Gooch opened the grocery store around 1909, taking up a store that had been recently vacated by Henry Uting. He built an expansion in 1914 and ran the grocery until his death in 1933.

General stores, like this unidentified one, were important to Boone County's villages. They carried a broad selection of necessary household items such as oatmeal, coffee, flour, and produce from local farmers. Often, general stores would trade or barter goods with farmers and other local business. By 1910, most general stores had disappeared, to be replaced with more specialized stores.

In 1890, William H. Piel started his grocery store when he was just 21 years old. He was well liked, personable, and knowledgeable, which contributed to the success of his business. By 1926, Piel employed over 45 employees and brought in over $5,000 in sales. The store also served as a trading center for farmers. Farmers brought milk, eggs, and produce to trade for produce they did not grow. In 1931, Piel's Grocery store won the *Collier's* magazine award for "most extraordinary grocery store" and was featured in a multipage article. The store remained a fixture in Belvidere until it closed in 1971.

Sarah Ames opened Mrs. A.T. Ames Millinery on South State Street in 1867. Millineries primarily sold women's hats; however, they often sold other goods such as scarves, jewelry, shirts, and shoes as well. Many of these items can be seen in the display windows. Ames successfully operated her millinery in Belvidere for over 40 years. She also served the public as a deputy sheriff.

Marvin C. Parsons originally started Parson's Casket Hardware Company in Elgin before moving the business to the site of the Big Thunder Manufacturing Company in Belvidere in 1909. Parson's sold casket handles, casket corners, religious goods, lodge emblems, and many other items. In 1913, the building burned down, and the company moved to its more familiar location at 424 Fairview Street. The business closed in 1982.

Plane Hardware was one of the most successful business operations in early Belvidere. John Plane immigrated to the United States from England in 1836 when he was 14 years old. His family initially moved to Geneseo, New York. After he completed an apprenticeship in 1842, he moved to Belvidere to start his own business on East Lincoln Avenue. Plane quickly found success selling items such as tools, wagon parts, stoves, cutlery, and other materials. His venture proved to be extremely successful and he eventually built a store block on the corner of State Street and Logan Avenue, which is now Alpine Bank. He successfully ran his hardware business in Belvidere for over 50 years before retiring in 1892.

The Julien House was a Belvidere landmark for approximately 100 years. Built in the 1850s, the hotel was located on the corner of Logan Avenue and Whitney Boulevard. The Julien House featured 60 rooms, two parlors, a kitchen, laundry, lodge, and small and large dining rooms. The hotel was a popular social center for many years, hosting weddings, banquets, and business meetings. Traveling salesmen and doctors frequently stayed at the hotel while conducting their business in town. In 1938, the porch area and fenced-in grass on the Whitney Boulevard side of the building were removed to make room for a Standard Oil gas station. The rest of the hotel was torn down in 1955.

This photograph depicts customers and employees of Dearth's Restaurant in downtown Belvidere. Started by three brothers—Louis, Leo, and Victor Dearth—the restaurant was located at 112 Logan Avenue. Due to its proximity to the factory, the restaurant was a popular coffee stop for workers from the National Sewing Machine Company. The family sold the restaurant in 1956 to Bob Wait. The building was later torn down in 1962.

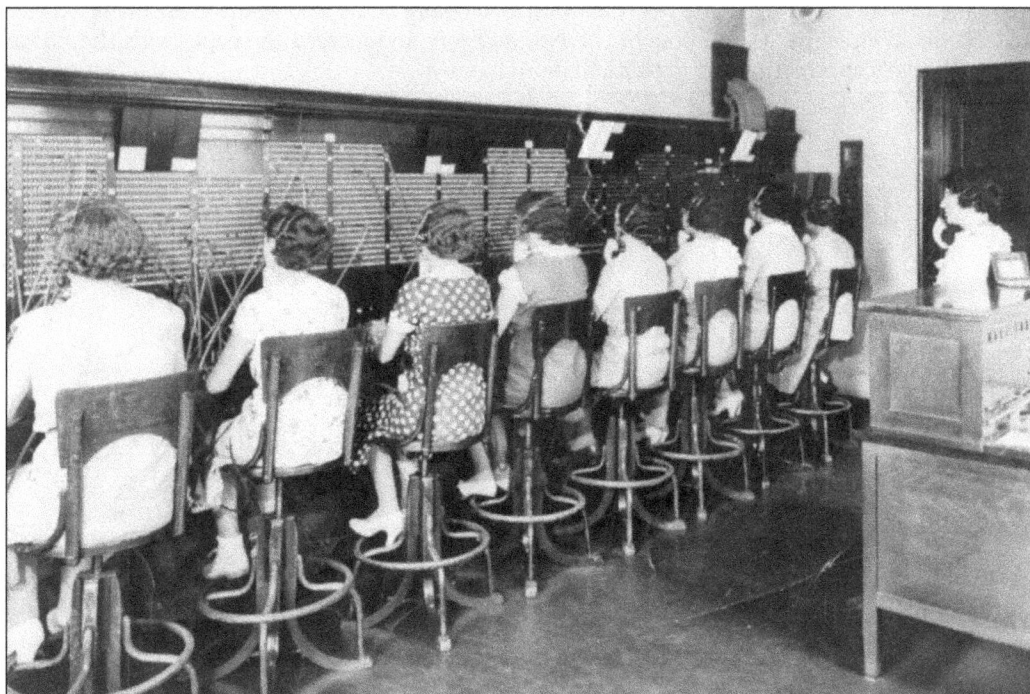

One option for women to work outside the home was at the switchboards of the Belvidere Telephone Company. The company was formed in the late 1800s by Josiah R. Balliet, William Marean, Omar H. Wright, and John Tripp. They started with 150 telephones in Belvidere. The company was located on the second floor of the Second National Bank.

Employees of the *Daily Northwestern* weekly newspaper pose here in front of their printing office, located on South State Street. The paper was first published in 1867 by Elisha H. Talbott. The company was then sold to Reuben W. Coon in 1870 before being sold again to Alson W. Keeler in 1888. In 1896, Frank Moran bought the *Northwestern* and merged the paper with the *Boone County Republican*, creating the *Republican-Northwestern*.

The *Belvidere Daily Republican* is Belvidere's most successful newspaper. Published daily, it was founded by Frank T. Moran in 1894 and its office was located at 112 West Pleasant Street. Shortly before issuing the first print, Moran purchased the *Daily Northwestern* from Alson Keeler; owning both papers reduced competition. At that time, the paper cost 3¢ per copy, 10¢ per week, or $4.50 for the year.

Frank Sewell (left) and Charles T. Sewell (right) were cashiers at the Second National Bank in Belvidere on South State Street. The bank was founded by several prominent business leaders in town and opened its doors on May 21, 1884, with assets at $186,000. The first customer was Isaac Witbeck. The bank later merged with the First National Bank in 1964.

The Poplar Grove Bank was founded in 1890 by Warren Webster and located on the west side of North State Street. It was destroyed in a massive fire that ruined 12 businesses in 1903. The bank was rebuilt and consolidated with Farmers National Bank in 1934. Throughout its history, the bank was victimized by four robberies, three of which were never solved.

George Spencer served as a blacksmith in Capron for over 50 years. He moved to Capron when he was 15 years old and started working as a blacksmith under Reuben J. Powell in 1887. Above, both men pose in front of their blacksmith shop. In 1905, Spencer bought out Powell to take ownership of the business. In the photograph below, Spencer (right) and his son Guy are shown working in the shop. Spencer continued working as a blacksmith until his death in 1939. In celebrating his 50 years as a blacksmith, the *Belvidere Daily Republican* printed the following on August 23, 1937, "To a friend Spencer confided one time that he never refused to repair a tool for a man simply because he didn't have money to pay for it."

In 1879, Frank June founded the June Manufacturing Company in Chicago, which specialized in making sewing machines. Barnabas Eldredge went into business with June in 1885. The following year, June moved his business to Belvidere to avoid the Chicago labor disputes. The first factory was a two-story building and employed 175 people. At that time, June served as president and Eldredge as vice president.

Following June's death in 1890, Eldredge took over as president and renamed the business the National Sewing Machine Company. The enterprise continued to expand, and by 1894, it employed over 700 people. The factory produced 75,000 sewing machines every year. In 1895, a large headquarters was built on South State Street. At its peak, the factory employed more than 2,500 people and took up nearly five blocks along Meadow Street.

In 1896, the National's milling department had 138 employees, some of whom are pictured above. Below is the factory's automatic-screw room. In 1896, the screw room employed 106 people. The National produced a number of products, including sewing machines, bicycles, washing machines, automobiles, and many other household items. The company was awarded three gold medals by the board of examiners for three sewing machine models—the Eldredge, Belvidere, and Seamstress—at the 1893 World's Fair in Chicago. During World War II, the factory switched to making bearings for the B-29 bomber. The factory closed its doors in 1954 and was demolished in 1966.

Five

COMMUNITY LIFE

As more people settled in Boone County, residents began to organize gathering places in the community. Early citizens worked to establish places of worship and entertainment, men's and women's clubs, and basic public services.

Religion was important to early Boone County residents. Before the formal construction of churches and congregations, many settlers held services in their own homes. Oftentimes, the sermons were given by visiting missionary priests and ministers traveling throughout the county. These small groups eventually developed into larger congregations, and formal churches were created. Many denominations formed churches here, including the Methodists, Baptists, Presbyterians, Catholics, Lutherans, and more. Nearly all of the early churches in the area have a unique and storied history, and many still exist today.

Gathering places offered socialization and entertainment to Boone County's citizens. People attended local venues such as the Majestic Theater, the Derthick Opera House, and later the Apollo Theater to see plays, concerts, and motion pictures. Residents also enjoyed meeting at the park and listening to music at the Big Thunder Park Bandstand. Clubs and organizations also offered social outlets. Men's and women's clubs such as the I.O.U. Club and the Rebekahs focused on improving the county as well as socialization.

Government services grew as the county did, and Belvidere is home to some of the most distinctive government buildings in the state. The Boone County Courthouse, built in 1854, still stands today, as does the former Belvidere Post Office, built in 1911. Fire and police protection, hospitals, a post office, and the Ida Public Library were just a few of the services created for the benefit of Belvidere and Boone County's residents.

The Boone County Courthouse (right), located on North Main Street across from Big Thunder Park, is the second-oldest courthouse in Illinois. In 1854, under the supervision of Allen C. Fuller, John Higby constructed the courthouse out of brick and stone for $18,508. At the time, it was considered one of the best-looking courthouses in the area. Despite its attractive appearance, many were concerned that it was located too far from the center of business. Although the courthouse contained a jail, it proved insufficient for the growing community's needs. In 1898, a new jail and sheriff's residence (left) was built for $12,000. The jail and sheriff's residence were torn down and replaced by the current public safety building in 1975.

The City of Belvidere was incorporated in 1882. This photograph, taken in the 1890s, shows an early glimpse of Belvidere's city council. In the early days, city council meetings were held in city hall on South State Street, which is now the fire station. The man in the center with white hair is Mayor Robert McInnes.

Poplar Grove was settled in the 1830s and became a village in 1895. It was originally part of both Boone and Caledonia Townships until Poplar Grove Township was formed in 1922. Pictured here is the 1906 village board. From left to right are (first row) Fred Shackell, William Willett, Wallace Manley, William Webster, and George Renne; (second row) a Mr. Willett, Joseph Long, Fred Slater, Charles Ableman, and Mayor Ira Moore.

This photograph is believed to be one of Chief William J. Richardson. Richardson came to Belvidere in 1860 when he was five years old, and he served Belvidere as a police officer for more than 50 years. He was known for his sound judgment and was well respected, even by those he arrested. His grandson Kenneth "Ted" Richardson also served as chief of police, from 1954 until 1977.

These members of the Belvidere Fire Department are standing in front of the south-side fire station. Notice the horse-drawn fire wagon in the foreground. The south-side fire station was built on Whitney Boulevard in 1899 for $9,000. The property later became Anderson Wholesale Pantry in 1937 and is now a parking lot. Belvidere's first fire company was organized in 1886, with R.J. Tousley serving as fire marshal.

Located on Warren Avenue and Second Street, American Hospital was the first hospital in Belvidere. Dr. George Tallerday opened the facility in 1880, and he was later joined by his son Dr. George Tallerday Jr. in 1901. The hospital housed 14 rooms; by 1906, it cared for more than 50 patients a year. The Tallerdays sold the hospital in 1910 to spend more time on their general practice.

At the urging of Dr. Robert W. McInnes, the Order of St. Joseph Sisters of Concordia, Kansas, established St. Joseph Hospital in 1900. The hospital served the community for nearly 100 years until it closed its doors in 1999. One of the most unique features of the hospital was the fog room used to treat upper respiratory infections. The fog was created by carefully controlling the humidity.

The Ida Public Library was formed in 1883 when Gen. Allen Fuller donated $5,000 to establish a library in memory of his daughter Ida. Earlier that year, Ida had died of consumption. Initially, the library was located on the second floor of city hall on South State Street. The current library building was constructed in 1913 for $17,500, partly funded by Pennsylvania steel baron Andrew Carnegie.

The Derthick Opera House was built by local entrepreneur and politician William H. Derthick in 1898. Its beautifully furnished interior could seat 1,200 people. The opera house was a venue for many theatrical productions, musical concerts, and moving pictures before it was destroyed in a fire in 1917. The Derthick Opera House was located on the current site of the Apollo Theater on North State Street in Belvidere.

The Belvidere Post Office is one of the most recognizable structures in town. It was built in 1911 in the Classical Revival style and designed by James Knox Taylor, who served as supervising architect of the US Treasury from 1897 to 1912. The building, including the land and furnishings, was constructed for $80,000. Frank T. Moran was one of the notable attendees at the cornerstone-setting ceremony, pictured immediately left of the crane. Moran was publisher of the *Belvidere Daily Republican* but also served the public as the postmaster. One of the most distinctive features of the post office is the rounded entry and broken pediment. The building was added to the National Register of Historic Places in 2000.

Located on First Street next to the Belvidere High School, the community building was constructed in 1939. The purpose of the building was to serve the expanding needs of both the high school and community. In 1938, a city vote was held to gain approval for construction of the new building. Once it was approved, Raymond Orput was selected as architect. The building's exterior is of Art Deco design and concrete construction. Inside, the community building contained a 1,500-seat auditorium, gymnasium, social center, and a dining room that could seat 500. Once completed, the total cost of the construction was $125,000, including the land. It was added to the National Register of Historic Places in 1997.

Initially known as the Public Square, Big Thunder Park is located across from the Boone County Courthouse. The park was named after legendary Potawatomie Indian chief Big Thunder, whose burial mound was said to be located near the courthouse. During summer evenings in the early 1900s, residents often gathered for concerts by local musicians. The works played included Russell Alexander's "From Tropic to Tropic" march and Franz von Suppé's *Poet and Peasant* Overture.

One of the prominent fraternal orders in Boone County was the Independent Order of Odd Fellows. Founded in Baltimore, Maryland, by Thomas Widley in 1819, the order believed in the principles of friendship, truth, and love. In 1847, Belvidere's Big Thunder Lodge No. 28 was instituted as a charter of the Independent Order of Odd Fellows, with Daniel Hornell serving as noble grand. The order met at 402 South State Street.

The Reverend Peterson of the Jefferson Prairie Church is pictured here with his family. As part of the Jefferson Prairie settlement in Manchester Township, the church's population was primarily Norwegian. In fact, the community was one of the earliest Norwegian settlements in America. The church still honors its Norwegian heritage with an annual smorgasbord.

The Capron Lutheran Church was first organized in 1844 by Norwegian settlers. The first service was conducted by Jefferson Prairie pastor Johannes Wilhelm Christian Dietrichson at the log cabin home of Lars Hove. Due to divisions within the congregation, four Lutheran churches were established by the late 1800s; in 1913, the different divisions settled their differences and reunited. The church pictured here was built in 1893.

The First Presbyterian Church started with 24 people meeting in log cabins in 1839. When the society built its first church in 1843, it was one of the first buildings in the county to be used exclusively for church purposes. As the congregation grew, the need for a bigger church was evident. In 1857, the current church was built for $18,000. The church exterior remains largely unchanged today.

Traveling priests from the Archdiocese of Chicago served Belvidere's early Irish Catholic population until the first St. James Catholic Church was built in 1864 on land donated by William Gilman. The current church building, which was recently expanded, was constructed in 1886 under Fr. Patrick McGuire and dedicated by Archbishop Patrick Freehan. A school and convent were established in 1909.

The first Methodist minister preached in Belvidere in 1838; from that time on, two Methodist congregations met until they formed the First United Methodist Church in 1885. A Romanesque Revival church building was erected on Logan Avenue in 1893 for $17,000. It was a fixture in Belvidere for over 100 years until it was torn down in 2007. Here, members of the First Methodist Church are gathered in 1936 to celebrate a patriotic holiday.

Founded in 1895, Camp Epworth served as a summer evangelistic meeting place for the Rockford District of the Methodist Episcopal Church. Accessible by rail in the summer months, the camp remained a popular meeting place for churches from Elgin to the Mississippi River until 1933. The 10-acre camp was located in a heavily wooded area on the northwest corner of Epworth Road and US 20.

The Willow Creek Presbyterian Church was founded in Caledonia Township by immigrants from Argyleshire, Scotland. The origin of the church can be traced to John Greenlee, who fled Scotland over unfair taxation. He was soon joined by other Scottish families, including the Reids, Andrews, and Pickens. The church was formally organized in 1844, and the present church was built in 1877 at a cost of $12,593.

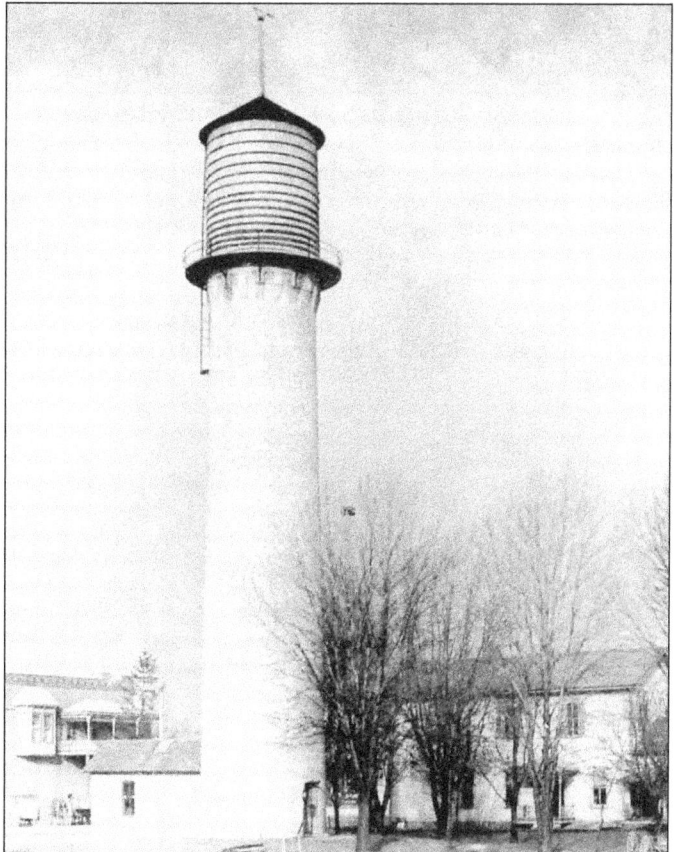

Though it no longer stands today, the Capron Water Tower is still remembered as a local Capron landmark. It was built in 1900 and stood 110 feet high. The water-storage tank held 28,000 gallons of water, which came from an 880-foot well. Airmail pilots in the 1930s used the tall structure as a route marker on their trips between Minneapolis and Chicago.

Dr. William Henry Pettit was born in 1851 and raised in Belvidere. After completing his medical studies, he moved to Cedar Rapids, Iowa, where he became a highly respected physician. Following his death in 1899, Dr. Pettit was buried in his hometown in Belvidere Cemetery. His widow, Emma Glasner Pettit, wanted to build a memorial for her husband. In 1905, she traveled to Chicago and commissioned world-renowned architect Frank Lloyd Wright to design a chapel in the Belvidere Cemetery near Pettit's final resting place. It was built in 1907 for $3,000. The chapel is an early example of Wright's Prairie School designs. It is also the only building ever designed by Wright for memorial purposes. The chapel required two significant restorations in 1977 and 2003 and was added to the National Register of Historic Places in 1978.

Six

GOOD TIMES

Life during the 19th and early 20th centuries was difficult. Hard work, disease, and loss were inevitable facets of life. Despite the hardships of daily living, Boone County's residents also knew how to have fun. Celebrations and social functions brought people together and strengthened the community. The best example of this is the Boone County Fair, which first started in 1855 and has become a much-anticipated annual event that draws thousands to Boone County.

National holidays were an excuse for everyone, from businessmen to farmers, to take a break and come together to celebrate; sporting events provided a healthy dose of competition and fun for players and onlookers alike. Boone County also had its cultural side, as evenings were often filled with concerts, lectures, and vaudeville shows. Clubs and organizations such as the local Granges were also popular ways for men and women to socialize. Despite its small size, Boone County was still connected to the excitement of national affairs. Celebrities such as Pres. Theodore Roosevelt and Red Cross founder Clara Barton were among the famous guests to visit here; in 1926, a Hollywood producer came and made a short silent film starring local actors called *Belvidere's Hero* that aired at the Apollo Theater.

On a local scale, friends and families had fun together, hosting parties, dancing, and going on picnics and camping trips. They also made sure to mark the milestones of weddings, birthdays, and anniversaries with pomp and circumstance. As one will see in this chapter, Boone County is full of fun stories, good memories, and people who knew how to have a good time.

It was a busy day in downtown Belvidere on the Fourth of July in 1865, three months after the end of the Civil War. According to the *Belvidere Standard* newspaper, about 5,000 to 6,000 people were present for the day's activities, which included patriotic speeches, music, and fireworks near the Courthouse Square.

A Christmas tradition that Belvidere remembers well is the community Christmas tree in the middle of South State Street, which often stood at 60 or 70 feet. The first downtown tree appeared in 1916 but became a yearly tradition in 1925. The lighting ceremonies in early December often included a visit with Santa. This memorable holiday tradition continued into the 1950s.

In 1928, Belvidere built a modern bridge across the Kishwaukee River at State Street. When completed, the State Street Bridge held the honor of being the widest usable bridge west of New York. Thousands attended the dedication ceremony on September 18, 1929, featuring speeches, a carnival, and a concert by the Belvidere High School band. The bridge stood for over 70 years until it was replaced in 2000.

Good times can always be had on a river. Although Boone County is landlocked, its chief waterway is the Kishwaukee River. The county is also full of creeks and streams such as the Piscasaw and Beaver. Living along these waterways provided Boone County residents like this unidentified gentleman with many forms of entertainment, including canoeing, fishing, trapping, and swimming.

During the 1920s and 1930s, summertime meant swimming at Marshall Beach, located at the bend of the Kishwaukee River by East Lincoln Avenue. The municipal beach opened on June 11, 1921, to great excitement. Amenities included a bathhouse, comfort stations, and slides; band concerts and water carnivals added to the fun. An exciting moment in Marshall Beach's history was when Johnny Weissmuller participated in a swimming race on July 19, 1922. A champion swimmer from Chicago, Weissmuller went on to win Olympic gold in the 1920s and play Tarzan in several Hollywood films during the 1930s and 1940s. River pollution eventually spelled the doom of the beach, which was deemed "dangerous and injurious to public health" in 1938. In response, the Belvidere Park District built a swimming pool in Belvidere Park, which opened on July 9, 1941.

This photograph captures a John Plane family picnic, complete with a large crowd and good food, sometime during the 1890s. The Plane house stood near the corner of South State Street and West Locust Street; Speckman and Associates now stands there. By the 1910s, that section of State Street had turned from a residential community into a business district.

Weddings have always been about family and friends as much as about the bride and groom. This extraordinary gathering in the farmyard of a home in Manchester Township is for a wedding in the Thorson family sometime in the 1890s. Rather than photographing the ceremony, this photographer captured the community of people that came together for events such as these.

World War I was a dark time for this nation. The declaration of peace on November 11, 1918, led to the "most jubilant, vociferous, noisiest day" in Belvidere history, according to the local newspaper. The National Sewing Machine Company's siren blew at 2:45 a.m. to announce the armistice, and people swarmed the streets, celebrating. A train engineer blew his horn from Caledonia and back to announce the news to the rural areas. On November 11, all businesses closed, and a victory parade was held through downtown Belvidere. The parade included thousands of marchers—local dignitaries, the drum corps, newspaper boys, Red Cross workers, schoolchildren, and residents in their cars. One little boy ran down the street yelling, "Daddy's coming home!" He was not the only one who was excited. All of Boone County was ready for its boys to return.

On October 8, 1902, thousands of people gathered in Belvidere to witness the queen's coronation—not the queen of England, but 22-year-old Maude Conley, queen of the Belvidere Carnival. A celebration and parade sponsored by the National Sewing Machine Company. Conley, who was presented with a diamond ring and rode in a special float with her "maids in waiting," won her title with more than 7,000 votes.

The bicycle craze hit the nation in the 1890s. Bicycling was especially popular with women, as it was considered an acceptable way for a lady to exercise. It also allowed social freedom in an age when most women were expected to work and socialize at home. Both men and women participated in this bicycle race near the corner of Lincoln and North State Streets on May 30, 1891.

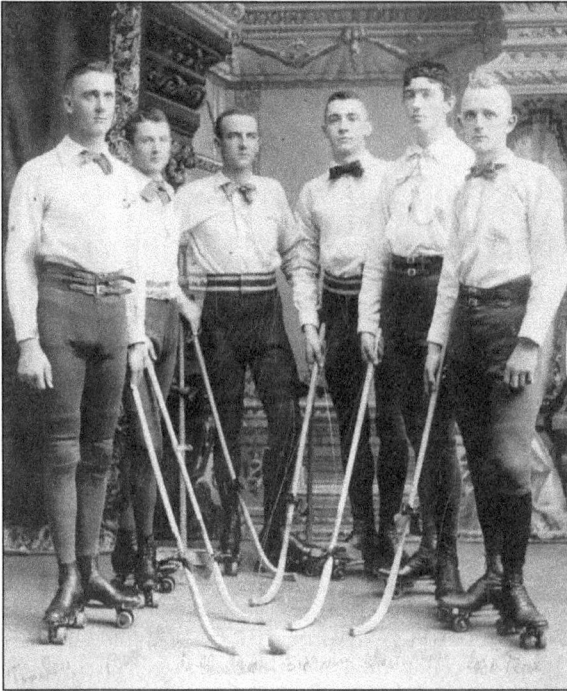

Local sports were a popular form of entertainment at the turn of the 20th century. The Belvidere hockey team poses for this photograph sometime in the late 1880s, complete with roller skates and hockey sticks. Pictured here, from left to right, are Herb Tousley, Bert King, Charles Peal, Sidney Sabin, Charles Parkhill, and George Peal.

Baseball games once ruled the summers in Boone County, as each town had one or more teams. Games were played at ballparks, in pastures, and at the fairgrounds. Local teams included the Caledonias, the Beaver Boys, the Poplar Grove Bluestockings, and the Belvidere Nationals. Here, the Capron Maroons pose at the Capron Village Park bandstand in 1908 around the time their team was organized.

On October 25, 1939, a crowd of 10,000 gathered on the Al Turnquist farm in Flora Township to watch the annual county corn-husking contest. Mildred Bye, fourth from left, held her title of reigning champion of the women's division by shucking 14.37 bushels—about 1,005 pounds—in the 30-minute period. Elizabeth Hawkey, third from left, came in second with 13.67 bushels. (Courtesy of Louise Hawkey Miles.)

People will certainly do interesting things for a good time. This group of Boone County fellows poses for a photograph to mark their participation in a beard-growing competition sometime in the early 1900s. The men are, from left to right, Will Keator, John Eldredge, Fred Gilman, Harry Pierce, and George Wallace.

DANCE HALL RAINBOW GARDENS

Rainbow Gardens was the best-known dance hall for miles around, according to the locals who remember it. Located on US Highway 20, halfway between Belvidere and Garden Prairie, Rainbow Gardens was built in 1924 by Ralph and Harry Dahlstrand. Big-band music, jazz bands, and orchestras from across the country provided hours of dancing and entertainment every summer. Headliners included local musicians as well as national stars such as Lawrence Welk, Wayne King, and Tiny Hill. On its busiest nights, Rainbow Gardens had more than 1,000 people in the hall. Rainbow Gardens especially attracted the younger crowds, who met up with friends and sweethearts there. The first 24-hour walkathon event came to Rainbow Gardens in 1933; people participated in this contest in the hopes of winning cash prizes. The dance hall's popularity peaked in the 1940s; it closed its doors in 1958 and was torn down in 1968.

The Belvidere City Band, shown here in 1910, formed in February 1904. The band gave concerts, played in local parades, and put on dancing parties throughout the area. From left to right are (first row) William Demus, Roy Slater, Walter Kenyon, Charlie Hance, Dick Bennett, Charles Harlow, and Lloyd Mench; (second row) Victor Johnson, Edward Slater, Harry Knight, Clyde Andrus, Gene Slocum, Angus Orford, William Pepper, and Bert Slack.

Radio was an instant phenomenon across the nation in the 1920s. Belvidere's first radio station, WOAG, went on air in November 1922 and was broadcast from the Apollo Theater, on North State Street. Programs featured local singers, speakers, and musicians. Competition soon appeared in the form of another station, WTAH, run by the Ferro Manufacturing Company. These stations did not last very long, but they brought Belvidere firmly into the radio age.

These Boone County gentlemen ham it up for the camera at a club picnic sometime in the early 1900s. They are, from left to right, (first row) Frank Goodrich, a Mr. Adams, Clarence Eldredge, John Kuppler, David M. Eldredge, William H. Moore, and William Waite; (second row) a Mr. Bishop, a Mr. Edwards, and David Patton; (third row) Frank W. Crain.

Many men came together to help William Ralston build his barn one summer day around the turn of the 20th century. Farm life in the 1800s was a difficult business, so family and neighbors relied on each other to succeed. Barn raisings, quilting bees, and other group events benefited the family and the community and made the work fun.

The Grange is a national organization comprised of local units and countywide units called the Pomona Granges. Boone County's Pomona Grange began in 1887. The many local Granges in Boone County were, and still are, active in supporting agriculture and their community. The Town Line Grange of Flora Township used its float to promote farming in this 1930s parade. (Courtesy of Louise Hawkey Miles.)

4-H has always been an integral part of growing up in Boone County. The 4-H group pictured here, the Newburg Clippers, organized in 1935 in Flora Township. Pictured are, from left to right, (first row) Richard Thomas, Lavern Matheson, Ruth Gustafson, and Margie Gustafson; (second row) Jack Sexauer, Gordon Fitch, Bill Thomas, Lawrence Matheson, Robert Gustafson, Ruth Menge, Celestia Fitch, and Charles Fitch. Louis Hawkey is holding the sheep. (Courtesy of Louise Hawkey Miles.)

In October 1855, the first Boone County Fair was held at Big Thunder Park, organized by the Boone County Agricultural Society. From 1867 until 1964, the fairgrounds were located on Appleton Road, at what is now Spencer Park. Then, as now, fair traditions centered on livestock judging and exhibits of domestic wares, art, and photography. Military displays, bicycle races, and plowing contests were also part of the fair fun.

Harness racing has been a popular fair event since 1855. The races feature horses pulling small two-wheeled carts called sulkies around a track. One popular local racing horse was Manager H., owned by William G. Hawkey. In 1905, Manager H. broke the world record for the fastest yearling colt, making Boone County home of a world champion.

Seven

HARD TIMES

The Great Depression hit Boone County as hard as it did nationally. The loss of farms, homes, and jobs accounted for hardships in every corner of the county. However, that event was not the only example of hard times here.

Times were difficult for the county's original settlers, most of whom lived off the land. Hard times began right away for the first farmers who had to turn the hard soil. Breaking the crust of the original prairie was a tough task until plows were invented to break up the soil. With few natural barriers to fend off disaster, prairie fires were common. John Greenlee's family settled in Scotch Grove in 1837. Years later, John's daughter Janette told of awakening to a "terrifying sight" that summer. The southern sky was ablaze, and a strong wind was blowing it their way. A sudden burst of rain ended the threat. Winters were hard; summers often dry. Two feet of snow fell on October 6, 1842, and roads did not open to normal traffic until the following April. Floods, droughts, and tornados added to the list of natural disasters.

Panics and economic downturns were felt locally. Some residents were forced to move to county poorhouses or farms. Blaine was the site of one poorhouse; the buildings of a county poor farm at the northwest corner of Orth and Beloit Roads stood until the turn of the 21st century.

Boone County endured two major conflicts in its first 100 years: the Civil War and World War I. The majority of local men fought in the 95th Infantry in the Civil War. Of its 279 casualties, 205 died from disease. Soldiers in World War I faced a similar fate, many dying from the Spanish flu epidemic of 1918. One of those was Johanna Habedank, a Red Cross nurse who died of the flu at Camp Grant. Despite the hardships, Boone County residents remained resilient, resolving to live and work for brighter days.

The winter of 1936 was one to remember. During January and February, the weather hovered at subzero temperatures for 32 days. Several giant snowstorms also hit the county in February. Drifts of 6 to 10 feet of snow blocked the roads, including Route 76, shown here. It took weeks to dig the roads out; residents were short on fuel and food and had to travel by bobsled through the fields.

Although the Kishwaukee River, called "Little Old Man River" by newspaper editor Frank Moran, appears to be a small river with narrow banks, its watershed reaches past Walworth and Sharon, Wisconsin, to six miles west of Elgin and south to Hampshire and Burlington. This photograph of the Kishwaukee was probably taken around 1900. Major floods occurred often until public works projects helped control the rising waters.

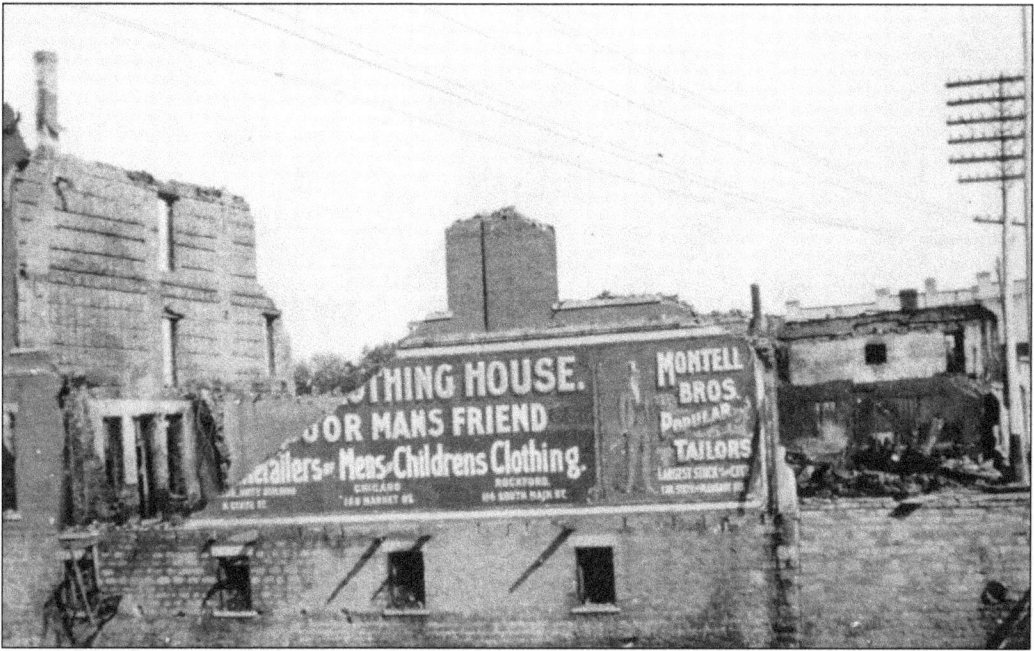

The Apollo Theater rose from the ashes of the Derthick Opera House, destroyed by fire on October 1, 1917. This photograph shows the ruins of the fire, a $50,000 loss; no cause was ever reported. The fire was spotted at 12:15 a.m., after the theater's weekly vaudeville show. It was the second time the theater burned to the ground; the first fire occurred in 1897.

Firefighters diligently spray water on this conflagration at South Belvidere High School. North Belvidere High School also was the site of a fire on December 2, 1908. Because school buildings of that era contained so much wood, fires were common and dangerous. Many school buildings had covered chutes extending from the second floor that allowed children to slide to safety in case of a fire.

Decoration Day, now known as Memorial Day, was first established nationally in 1868, soon after the end of the Civil War. Boone County honored its fallen soldiers every year with downtown parades and ceremonies at county cemeteries, where soldiers' graves were decorated with flowers. Local veterans' posts also strewed flowers on the Kishwaukee River in memory of soldiers who died on the water. Congressman Charles Fuller, seated on the far right in the photograph below, was a frequent speaker at Belvidere's Decoration Day observances. Though Decoration Day began to honor the "heroic struggle" of the Civil War, the day gained new meaning after the devastation of World War I, when veterans of both wars came together each May to honor their fallen comrades.

Boone County was well represented in the Civil War. In the 95th Volunteer Infantry regiment, nearly 300 men lost their lives to battle or disease. Many more survived, and this photograph from May 1925 includes the last 21 of the county's war veterans. The GAR commander, William Henry Tuttle, stands third from right in the front row.

Eight figures in hooded KKK robes lay a bouquet and cross on the grave of a local man at his funeral in the Belvidere Cemetery in December 1923. The Ku Klux Klan was very active nationally and locally during the 1920s, promoting anti-Catholic, anti-Jewish, and anti-black doctrines. The Belvidere Klan put on parades and programs to champion its cause. Its popularity ended by the late 1920s.

These soldiers in Company M of the 33rd Division, also known as Belvidere's Own, were photographed in a French village during World War I. Of the many Boone County servicemen who gave their lives, eight were from Company M, including Merle Clark, who died at Metz on October 24, 1918, just 18 days before the armistice. Three other Belvidere doughboys from Company M died earlier that month.

Matthew Becker was born in Chicago but raised in Belvidere. During World War I, then known as the Great War, he joined Company M of the 33rd Division. He married and raised a family in Belvidere while working for the Service Company and Northern Illinois Gas Company. He died at the age of 59 in 1956.

A crowd estimated at 15,000 gathered at Big Thunder Park for the dedication of the Soldiers and Sailors Memorial on October 15, 1910. The gathering was one of the largest in county history. The memorial, which cost $9,000, was built to honor those who fought in the Civil War. Ironically, a former official of the Confederacy was among those in attendance.

Memorial Park in Poplar Grove was built to honor those who fought in World War I. It is located in the center of the village, south of the former railroad tracks. The monument reads, "In honor of those who responded to their country's call from Poplar Grove, Illinois, in the Great War, 1914–18." It also honors veterans of World War II, Korea, and Vietnam.

Hundreds of children from Belvidere schools took part in this "Local Option" parade through downtown Belvidere on April 4, 1908. Years before Prohibition became the law of the land, voters approved the local option to ban liquor sales in town, including those at pharmacies. The police chief led this temperance parade, which stretched for blocks and featured 15 floats. One wagon carried 40 children, and most of the city's churches took part as well. Notice the signs "Do It Now," and "Follow the Gleam," a phrase attributed to Frances Willard, the founder of the Woman's Christian Temperance Union. On her deathbed in 1898, Willard, a noted activist, is reported to have said, "I am Merlin, and I am dying, but I will follow the gleam." Although this march was peaceful, another gathering later that week drew protesters, who threw eggs and other objects at participants. The local option law passed on April 7, forcing saloonkeepers to close their doors within 30 days.

At right is the only known photograph of Hairbreadth Harry, the King of the Hobos. He was born James Joseph Moan on a farm in Spring Township in June 1881 and rode the rails after leaving his family at 17 years old. He was twice crowned King of the Hobos by his peers in Adair, Iowa, and was known for his poetry and love of walking backward. He also wore inner tubes or burlap sacks tied to his feet, as seen in this photograph. Hairbreadth Harry, along with his other "Knights of the Road," often frequented Hobo Island, seen below, located on the Kishwaukee River just off the railroad tracks east of Belvidere. It was a popular gathering place for hobos, tramps, and other wandering men during the Great Depression.

On November 5, 1932, Pres. Herbert Hoover (left) and his wife, Lou Henry Hoover, stopped at the Belvidere train depot to promote his presidential election campaign. The country was in the midst of the Great Depression, and the Republican incumbent Hoover was campaigning against Democrat Franklin D. Roosevelt. Hoover delivered a seven-minute speech to a festive crowd of 10,000 people, serenaded by the Belvidere High School band's rendition of "Stars and Stripes Forever." Hoover had won Illinois in the 1928 election against Al Smith but had not responded well to the economic downturn that affected millions in the United States. Nominated for a second term, Hoover crossed the country seeking reelection and made this whistle-stop in Belvidere, where he was immensely popular. In the 1932 election, Hoover won 70 percent of the vote in Boone County. However, that was not enough, as Roosevelt carried the state with 55 percent of the vote and overwhelmingly won the election.

Eight

SCHOOL DAYS

Boone County was only settled for three years when Lydia Lawrence of Bonus Township started a free school under an oak tree for area children. The first official school in Boone County was the Newton Academy, a private school for boys, which opened in 1838. The school stood in Belvidere, one block from Courthouse Square at what is now 418 Hancock Street. The academy was operated by several teachers over the years, including Prof. Seth S. Whitman and Arthur Fuller, grandfather of architect Buckminster Fuller. The school closed in 1852, and the building was converted to a barn that later burned down.

From those early beginnings, education continued to be a priority for Boone County's citizens. Public, tax-funded schools in Belvidere were founded during the 1850s both north and south of the river. The North Belvidere School began in 1854, in a stone building on the Courthouse Square that could accommodate 400 elementary and high school scholars. The South Belvidere School, located on Pearl Street, was established in 1857. In 1912, the North and South High Schools consolidated to create one Belvidere High School. Belvidere's earliest elementary schools—Lincoln, Logan, Perry, and Washington—also developed in the early decades of the 1900s.

Boone County was once home to over 80 rural schools divided into districts. The rural schools taught all grades in one room, employing young unmarried women as teachers. They also functioned as community centers for the rural towns in Boone County, hosting basket socials, meetings, and other community events. The rural schools were consolidated into two districts in 1948; District 100 covered the Belvidere area and southern Boone County, while District 200 encompassed northern Boone County.

Boone County's schools have always offered more than just reading, writing, and arithmetic. As this chapter demonstrates, schools have been cornerstones of the community and continuing sources of pride for students, faculty, and alumni.

Carpenter School, located in Manchester Township, was first built in 1864 out of logs but replaced in 1871. This photograph shows Carpenter students in 1891, some of whom have been identified as Ruby Carpenter, Maude Haskins, Irene Wells, Anna Schintcke, Mary Bogardus, Grace Peacock, and Ruth Colvin, who served as teacher. After the rural schools were consolidated in 1948, the building was renovated into a house.

The White Pigeon schoolhouse is shown here during the winter of 1886. It was built in 1860 on the Samuel Happer farm, at the intersection of Spring Creek and Olson Roads. The teacher, Wallace Manley, is standing at the far left. It is not known where the name White Pigeon came from, but one story says it referred to the fair-haired students who looked like little white pigeons.

On June 10, 1897, the schoolchildren of Blaine School and their teacher pose for a photograph. Built in 1857, the schoolhouse was located in the town of Blaine in Leroy Township next to the Methodist church. The identities of the schoolchildren are unknown, except for the two girls who have been circled. They are sisters named Edith and Eva Farmer.

Scriven School of Spring Township was located on Scrivin Road, south of Davis School Road and across from James Scrivens's farm. The schoolhouse was built in 1874 and functioned as a school until 1947. Some of Scriven's teachers throughout the years included Martha (Behling) Count, Lucille Dewan, and Hazel (Vowles) Wesson. Pictured here are the teacher and the entire student body of the Scriven School in 1911.

On May 10, 1933, the Avery School of Flora Township became the first rural school in Boone County dedicated as a superior school, due to its excellent facilities and student work. Of over 10,000 rural schools in Illinois at that time, only 175 had been so named. Francis G. Blair, state superintendent of schools, presented the school with a plaque at a public dedication program. (Courtesy of Louise Hawkey Miles.)

Lawrenceville School in Bonus Township held the distinction of being the first free public school in Boone County since Lydia Lawrence had taught students on the Lawrence property in 1838. A few schoolhouses were built in Lawrenceville over the years until the official schoolhouse, shown here, was built in 1860, at the intersection of Lawrenceville and Russellville Roads.

High school classes began meeting in Capron in the mid-1880s in the Capron village school, offering a three-year course to students. Pictured here is the graduating class of 1907 and the school principal. From left to right are (first row) Alma Wolfram, principal James R. Skiles, and Mary Lambert; (second row) William Smith, June Rolandson, Ellen Georgeson, and Alfred Stimes. In 1916, Capron voters established a new high school district to offer a four-year high school curriculum. The "modern and commodious" new high school was dedicated on November 2, 1917. Since the district included part of McHenry County, the school's official title was the Boone-McHenry Township High School, but it was mostly known as the Capron High School. This school served students until 1957, when the northern Boone County schools were consolidated and a new high school was built.

The first public school in Belvidere was a stone structure built in 1851 next to the courthouse on Main Street. Classes at the Belvidere Union School taught elementary, intermediate, and high school students. In 1895, it was replaced with a brick building, pictured here. The new school boasted 10 schoolrooms and modern lighting and heating. An official high school was established on the top floor. The first principal of North Belvidere High School was John C. Zinser. After the high schools consolidated in 1912, the building became an elementary school known as Lincoln School. Lincoln School closed in 1999, and the building was demolished in 2007. In the photograph below, the teachers of the North Belvidere School pose in one of the classrooms.

The first South Belvidere school (left) was built in 1857 at the corner of Pearl and Pleasant Streets and known as the Pearl Street School. Both grade school and high school students were taught there. In 1894, Garfield School (right) was constructed at Pearl and First Streets to accommodate growing class sizes. In 1916, the Pearl Street School was replaced by a new high school building. The Garfield School building still stands today.

These South Belvidere students are, from left to right, (first row) Callie McKenna, Jim O'Brien, George Bishop, and Roy Boyce; (second row) Robert Melville, May Difford, Leah Miller, Paul Pritchard, Fred Sands, and Jay Harding; (third row) Olive Lewis, Lola Johnson, Audrey Smith, Hazel Horner, Maud Adams, and Ella Riddle; (fourth row) Olive Walquist, Grace Garner, Tressa Murrin, Flossie Silvius, and Earl Walley; (fifth row) Nettie Still, Art Atkins, Earl Drake, June Holmes, Jessie Bowley, Ethel Packard, Mae Delavergne, Alta Hamblet, ? Gannon, Winnifred Brook, Lilly Penning, Clarence Thornton, and George Barnes.

Two high schools became one in 1912 when Belvidere's high schools were consolidated. The school building on Pearl Street, built in 1916, still features largely in the memories of many high school graduates. The school was considered quite modern for its day, with an auditorium, library, chemistry laboratory, and individual lockers. This building served as the high school until 1966 and was listed in the National Register of Historic Places in 1997.

In the early 1900s, the Playground Movement taught that children needed fresh air and exercise during the school day. For this reason, the Belvidere School Board decided to raise funds to build a playground at the Logan School. Opened in June 1914, it served as both a school and public playground, with supervised playtimes throughout the summer. Logan School, built in 1896, still stands on Logan Avenue. (Courtesy of Ida Public Library.)

The Belvidere High School offered its students many opportunities to engage in extracurricular activities, including Booster Club, band, the *Bel-Hi* school paper, plays, and the *Belvi* yearbook committee. These young men are members of the 1939–1940 B Club, which was committed to promoting clean athletics and enforcing training rules. Bob Lear, who later owned Lear's Jewelry, is in the second row, fourth from left.

The Caledonia High School began in 1922 after the Caledonia, Cummings, and Morgan rural school districts were consolidated. In the winter of 1922, Caledonia residents contributed $300 to purchase equipment for the athletic program. The Caledonia High School basketball team was undefeated in its early years; the 1924–1925 team, pictured here, was "the greatest team" the school ever had, according to a November 1924 newspaper article.

"Send One Boy to Denver" was the slogan during May 1929 in support of the Belvidere High School band. The band, led by Clarence F. Gates, won the Illinois state band championship in April of that year, giving it the chance to compete nationally in Denver, Colorado. Belvidere quickly rallied to raise the $5,000 necessary for the trip by sponsoring dances, church suppers,

D CONTEST - DENVER, COLORADO - MAY 1926

bake sales, and more. Residents and local organizations also made monetary pledges. A large crowd gathered on May 21 to send off all 72 members of the band as they boarded the train for Colorado. To the delight of Belvidere residents, the band won first honors in its class in Denver on May 26.

One of two parochial schools in Belvidere, the St. James School on Logan Avenue was dedicated on November 6, 1910. In this photograph of the eighth grade graduating class of 1929 are, from left to right, (first row) Robert Borsberry, Pat Hamill, Hazel Paulson, Ruth Lorenz, Helen McMahon, Mary Durkee, Roland Shea, and Frank Conley; (second row) Marguerite Stapleton, Viola Moore, Charles Meyers, Father Ronald French, Vincent Stapleton, Mary Hamill, and Mary Donovan. French was the assistant pastor at St. James Catholic Church in the 1920s.

Immanuel Lutheran Church, organized in 1869, first opened a school in 1886. In 1905, the congregation donated almost $6,000 to build a new schoolhouse at 418 Boone Street; it was officially dedicated on September 9, 1906. The Immanuel Lutheran School closed in 1920 due to lack of students but was used for Sunday school classes until the school reopened in 1953.

Nine

ON THE MOVE

Many Boone County towns and villages, including Belvidere, Garden Prairie, Caledonia, Poplar Grove, and Capron, owe their early development to transportation. The stagecoach line from Chicago to Galena was the first thoroughfare through the county, with stops in Garden Prairie and Belvidere. Following the stagecoach road, the Galena & Chicago Union Railroad came through Boone County in 1851; the railroad was consolidated into the Chicago & North Western Railway in 1864. Three railway lines once snaked through Boone County. The first went northwest from Chicago to Freeport with stops in Belvidere and Cherry Valley. Another ran east-west from Kenosha, stopping in Capron and Caledonia. The last line traveled north-south through Herbert, Belvidere, and Caledonia. Due to the railroad, small towns grew larger, while towns that were bypassed by the railroad, like Newburg and Russellville, slowly disappeared. By the end of the century, Boone County's major towns were travel hubs that provided abundant travel options within and beyond Illinois's borders.

Before modern transportation, people primarily depended on horse-drawn vehicles. Fields were plowed, goods were delivered, and fires were fought with the help of horses; people needed horses and carriages to take them where they wanted to go. The advent of the automobile in the first decade of the 20th century changed society's dependence on the horse, thus changing the landscape of the county's cities and homes. Roads were widened and paved to accommodate the new vehicles. Garages replaced carriage houses, and blacksmiths became mechanics. Boone County became home to a wide array of family-owned and -operated service stations, automobile dealers, and mechanics, some of whom are still in business today.

Changes in transportation over time have altered how people travel, led to the transfer of more goods, bolstered the economy, and shortened distances. Boone County's history is just one more example of how advances in transportation affect society on both national and local levels.

Borden's Condensed Milk Company opened in Belvidere in 1895 and consisted of a factory and icehouses on three acres of land. Like other dairies, Borden's picked up milk from area farmers and delivered ice, milk, and cream to its customers daily. The factory, which operated until 1924, was located where Dean Foods now stands on Meadow Street.

Towns and villages before the 1920s contained a variety of businesses focused on the care and upkeep of horses, wagons, carts, and carriages. Livery stables provided horses, teams, and wagons for hire as well as boarding services for privately owned horses. This unidentified livery stable was located in Caledonia.

Arthur J. Humphrey opened his first wagon shop on South State Street in 1897 after apprenticing with his uncle for four years. By 1900, business was booming, so he built a new shop on Leonard Court behind the site of the current fire station on South State. Humphrey's provided blacksmithing services and also manufactured, repaired, and painted wagons and carriages. It operated until 1926.

Imagine getting warm bread and pastries delivered right to the door. During the 1800s, many businesses, including local bakeries, offered delivery services to make shopping more convenient for their customers. The Belvidere City Bakery was opened by Henry F. Bowley around 1887 on South State Street. It operated for about 10 years, after which Bowley opened a popular restaurant.

The village of Garden Prairie did not exist until the Galena & Chicago Union Railroad came through Bonus Township in 1851. When a train station was built to the east of Ames Tavern, a town sprang up around it. The settlement had no name until someone stepped off the train one day and pronounced, "It looks like a garden on the prairie." Pictured here is station agent Charles Kiester.

These Chicago & North Western Railway employees posing on the platform of the rail yards are, from left to right, John Haack, John Meyers, Thaddeus Kinzie, William Johannes, Charles Schultz, George Comery, Christian Hagemeister, Jake Fassler, Fred Frank, Ludwig Busse, unidentified, Alfred Edwards, Barney Keating, Charles Johannes, William Feldman, Ernest Wheeler, Harry Hemmens, Robert Anderson, and Fred Bull. (Courtesy of Louise Hawkey Miles.)

Belvidere's iconic passenger depot was built in 1897 near Main Street, on the north side of the railroad tracks. It was the city's second depot; the first was an old shed built in 1851. The depot was one of the busiest centers of the city. Between 1917 and 1930, nine passenger trains stopped daily. The depot is now just a memory, as it was razed in 1966.

The oldest building still standing in Poplar Grove is intimately tied to the town's railroad history. The Poplar Grove Hotel was built in 1856 and served both travelers and railroad employees; a 1900 advertisement describes its 14 sleeping rooms, billiard hall, barroom, and dining hall. Dances were often held there as well. Proprietors over the years included Ira and Addie Webster and Edward and Min Clark.

Located near the Caledonia depot, the Chamberlain Hotel served hungry travelers, local residents, and the railroad crews with good food and great hospitality, making the hotel a popular place for miles around. Catherine "Kate" Chamberlain bought the Montayne House in March 1879 and changed the name. She had moved from Chicago to Caledonia to join her brother Colin Lang, a Caledonia blacksmith and Civil War veteran. Kate ran the hotel while her husband, William, operated a saloon on the lower level. After William left her in the 1890s, Kate ran the establishment alone with the help of her daughters Maggie and Katie. The Chamberlain was so popular that incoming trains wired the station agent with the number of passengers aboard so Kate could prepare enough food. After Kate's death in 1929, her daughters continued to operate the hotel. Though local historical groups tried to save it, the building was demolished in the mid-1970s.

Caledonia became a station along the Galena & Chicago Union Railroad around 1853. In 1861, the Chicago & North Western Railway's Kenosha-Rockford route came through Caledonia as well, making Caledonia a busy rail junction. Soon, Caledonia became the scene of heavy freight and passenger rail traffic, including famous visitors like the Ringling Bros. Circus and Pres. William Taft. Here, a passenger train chugs past the Chamberlain Hotel and the depot.

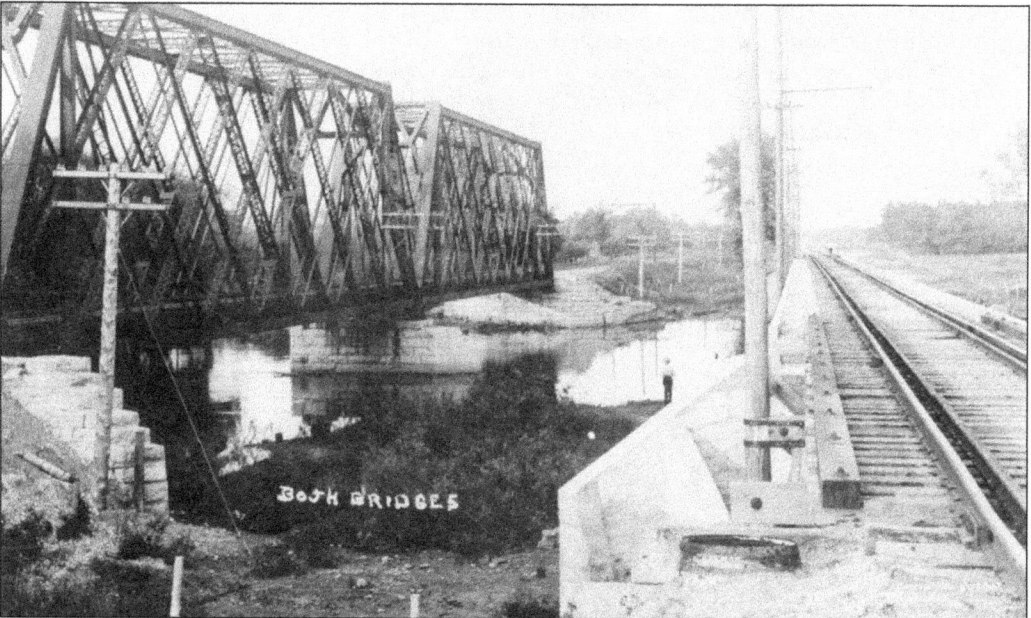

Two abandoned bridges span the Kishwaukee River and its tributary Coon Creek, north of the Bel-Mar Country Club. The first is an iron Chicago & North Western Railway Bridge known as the 2½ Mile Bridge. The second is the concrete Elgin-Belvidere Interurban Line Bridge, built in 1906 and active until 1930. The bridges and surrounding areas were popular with residents who often came to hunt, fish, hike, and picnic.

Between 1900 and 1915, interurban lines were a valuable service. In an era before improved roads and the proliferation of the automobile, the interurban allowed rural residents to travel greater distances and gain access to the offerings of urban centers. Two different interurban lines once came through downtown Belvidere: the Rockford and Belvidere (R&B) line, beginning in 1901, and the Elgin-Belvidere (E&B) line. Passengers could connect from one line to the other, essentially traveling straight from Rockford to Chicago. On February 13, 1906, the first streetcar on the E&B line trundled down Logan Avenue past the Methodist church, as shown above. The station for both lines was located on Pleasant Street, between Pearl and South State Streets. Both the R&B and the E&B lines ceased operation on March 9, 1930; by that time, automobiles had rendered their services unnecessary.

Standing in front of the Triangle Garage in this 1911 photograph are, from left to right, Leslie Porter, Walter Fry, a Mr. Lovejoy, and Tom Beckington, the garage's owner. The Triangle was Belvidere's first automobile garage, established around 1908. Beckington was well known as an expert mechanic. The business moved to Logan Avenue in 1916, but the building still stands near the corner of Pearl and West Pleasant Streets.

This unidentified Boone County gentleman is enjoying a drive in his runabout car. A runabout was an open car with no doors, roof, or windshield; it sported one seat and featured smaller wheels, as seen here. They were popular until about 1915. This man's automobile was manufactured in 1901 and is either a Ford Quadricycle—Henry Ford's first automobile design—or an Oldsmobile Curved Dash.

In 1894, the National Sewing Machine Company began manufacturing bicycles after purchasing the Freeport Bicycle Manufacturing Company and moving it to Belvidere. In short time, the Belvidere wheels became known for their beauty and strong construction. In its first year of manufacturing, the National sold 10,000 bicycles. It produced a number of models for men and women into the 1930s.

In 1903, the National Sewing Machine Company tried its hand at a new and innovative form of transportation—the automobile. Two models were developed and manufactured between 1903 and 1906. The Eldredge Runabout could seat two passengers, had a three-speed transmission, and sold for $750. The 1904 Eldredge Tonneau seated five passengers and sold for $2,000—a modern touring car at a competitive price. One of the Runabouts is on display at the Boone County Historical Museum.

"A motorcycle doesn't eat like a horse." So begins a 1913 advertisement for Walter E. Lincoln's Harley-Davidson dealership at 205 South State Street. In the late 1800s and early 1900s, motorcycles, like automobiles, were viewed as cost-efficient and time-saving alternatives to horse-drawn vehicles. Lincoln, who was also a rural mail carrier, sold motorcycles at his establishment until about 1920. This building still stands today.

In 1916, Clinton C. Hendrickson and Sidney Sears opened this garage, which repaired cars and sold Ford and Chevrolet vehicles, in Garden Prairie. Hendrickson bought out Sears in 1919, the same year several thieves took off with tires and other accessories valued at $75. He continued in the automobile trade until 1922, when he sold the garage to take over his father's grocery store.

With the advent of automobiles, a new business opportunity opened: the filling station or service station. Harry Cohoon, like other enterprising locals, opened a filling station on his property on US Route 20 near the corner of Van Epps Road in the mid-1930s. Cohoon sold Standard Oil gasoline at his station, which he operated until 1948. The building still stands today.

This Belvidere service station, opened around 1922, was located at 130 East Lincoln Avenue. It was owned by A.B. James, who operated a string of gas stations in the area. James also published an advertisement column called Oil News in the *Belvidere Daily Republican* to inform readers about car care and advertise his business. James sold his stations and moved to Rockford in 1926.

Sometime before 1883, Joseph H. Fellows, a plumber and entrepreneur, opened a boathouse on the Kishwaukee River on the Doty Flats, behind what is now the Dari-Ripple ice-cream stand. The structure pictured here was rebuilt in 1887 after a devastating flood. The boathouse rented canoes and boats to pleasure-seekers. During winter months, it was also used as a warming shelter for ice-skaters out on the river.

Eight years after the Wright brothers made their historic first flight at Kitty Hawk, the budding international world of aviation came to Boone County. The event was called Aviation Day and was held on October 18, 1911, at the Boone County Fairgrounds. Nationally renowned flyer Lincoln Beachey came for the event, dazzling the crowds with flight demonstrations in his newfangled airplane.

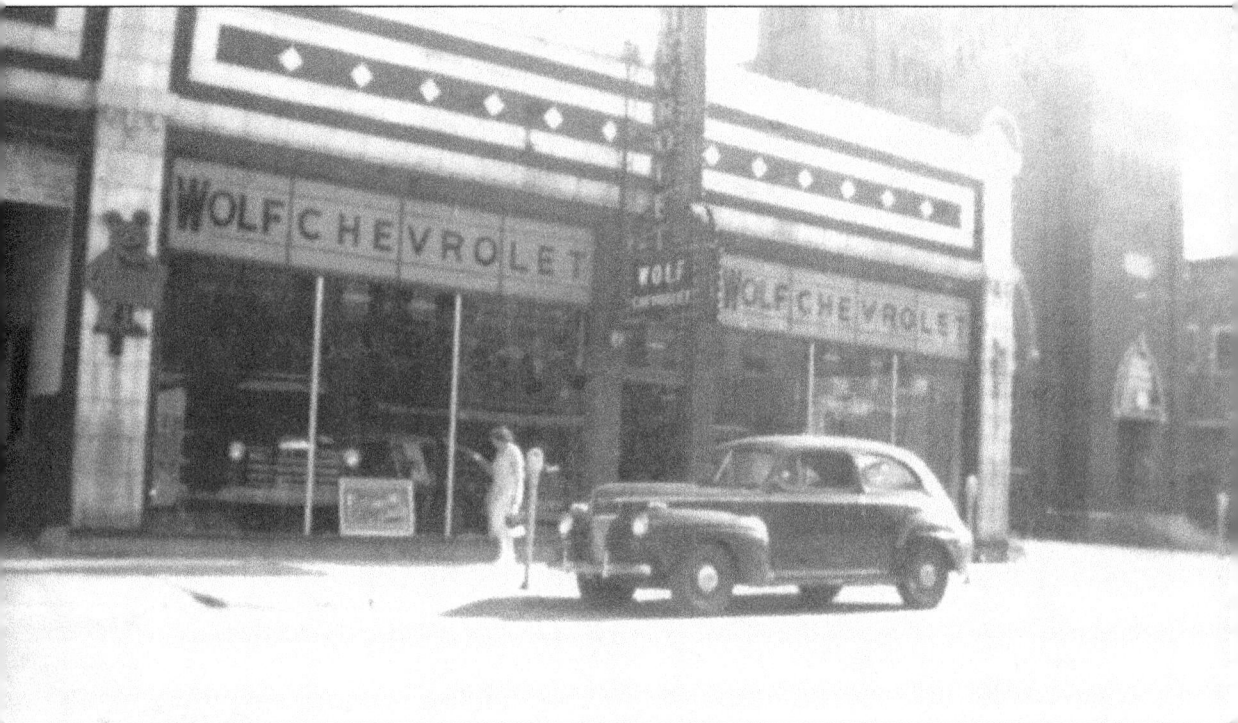

The first mention of Clarence "Doc" Wolf in Belvidere is an April 23, 1924, newspaper article. It reads, "The Chevrolet agency for this territory has just been taken over by R.V. Flynn and C.J. Wolf, enterprising young business men who have just arrived here from Dubuque, Iowa." Their dealership, called Belvidere Motor Sales, was located at 517 Whitney Boulevard. In the 1920s, Whitney Boulevard was dubbed "automobile row" due to the many garages and dealers located there, including Simon Motor Company and Manley Motors—which today is the second-oldest Ford dealership in the country. Wolf renamed the dealership Wolf Chevrolet Sales soon after Flynn left the business. In 1928, the dealership relocated to the corner of Logan and Whitney Avenues, where it continued to operate until 1964. Unlike many other businesses, Wolf Chevrolet weathered the Great Depression and prospered into the 21st century. The first truck Wolf ever sold, a 1924 Chevrolet, is now on display at the Vintage Wings & Wheels Museum in Poplar Grove. (Courtesy of the Wolf family.)

ABOUT THE BOONE COUNTY HISTORY PROJECT COMMITTTEE

Joanna Dowling is an artist and cultural historian. She is an avid writer and photographer and a lover of the outdoors.

Mike Doyle is a retired journalism teacher who has written two other books on Boone County history. He enjoys cooking, especially recipes from his Italian family.

Judy Ernest and her husband, Maurice, live in Belvidere, where they raised three sons. They volunteer at the Boone County Historical Museum, and Judy serves on the board.

Mike Frederiksen creates and writes exhibits for the Poplar Grove Wings and Wheels Museum. He is passionate about history, heritage, and preservation.

Jillian Fuller is the local history and genealogy librarian at Belvidere's Ida Public Library. Besides writing, she enjoys reading, cooking, history, and travel.

Douglas Heuer grew up in the Capron area and has a bachelor's degree in psychology and a master's in computer science. He is married to Teresa and has two children, Heather and Michael.

David Kummerow is dedicated to historic preservation and is a member of the Belvidere Historic Preservation Commission. He and his wife live in a restored 1897 Victorian Belvidere home.

Kathy J. Miller is a planner with the Belvidere-Boone County Planning Department, the liaison for the Belvidere Historic Preservation Commission, and enjoys watercolor painting and gardening.

Belinda and Lloyd Roberts are lifelong Boone County residents. They are teachers and avid gardeners who have a love of local history.

Visit us at
arcadiapublishing.com

www.ingramcontent.com/pod-product-compliance
Lightning Source LLC
Chambersburg PA
CBHW080559110426
42813CB00006B/1342

* 9 7 8 1 5 3 1 6 7 1 2 9 7 *